THE ULTIMATE WEAPON
IS NO WEAPON

THE ULTIMATE
WEAPON
IS NO WEAPON

Human Security and the
New Rules of War and Peace

SHANNON D. BEEBE and
MARY KALDOR

PublicAffairs
New York

Set in 11.5 point Electra by the Perseus Books Group

Cataloging-in-Publication data for this book is available from the Library of
Congress
LCCN: 2010922745
ISBN-13: 978-1-58648-823-9

10 9 8 7 6 5 4 3 2 1

*To the rangers of Virunga National Park and
other unknown heroes of human security.*

CONTENTS

1

Introduction

As we were finishing this book, Shannon Beebe began his posting as a U.S. military attaché in Angola, Africa. We tried to discuss the final chapters by phone but Beebe's phone was always busy. The reason was an unfolding humanitarian crisis in Cabinda, in the north of Angola, where thousands of people had fled from neighboring Democratic Republic of the Congo (DRC).

"I'm just begging someone," said Beebe when Mary Kaldor finally reached him, "if I can find an airplane so that I can fly up there and see for myself . . . the reality is that the rains have started and there are over 30,000 people who don't have any kind of shelter, or access to food, water. . . . And you just sit here and scratch your head and go, 'How does this happen so quickly?'

"And of course, once again, we're poorly situated to do anything about it because we have waited too long, we don't know any of the players up there, and now the Americans try coming in and it's Johnny-come-lately saying, 'We're here to help.' It doesn't work that way. People don't believe us. We haven't introduced ourselves to the population up there—so why, they wonder, are we suddenly interested now? One of the things I'm talking about with AFRICOM [U.S. African Command] and anyone else who will listen is that we cannot have a perceived policy by proxy or that is event-driven, because it makes no sense—it's like watching a kids' soccer match: everyone's chasing whatever the crisis du jour is. There's no organization, no priorities, no reliability like this.

"Folks here are skeptical about why a military guy is so interested in doing these things that are so traditionally a development type of activity. They're just not used to hearing words like this come from a military guy; they want to know what the catch is."

We have been developing the ideas in this book for more than a decade, initially independently, now collaboratively. We each had parallel experiences in the conflicts of the 1990s. During the wars in the Balkans, Kaldor was the chairperson of the Helsinki Citizens' Assembly, a non-governmental organization (NGO) working on peace and human rights that had branches throughout Bosnia and Herzegovina, when at the same time Beebe was stationed in Germany preparing troops to be sent to Bosnia and Herzegovina.

We both saw that the distinction between "battle space" and "humanitarian space" was dissolving rapidly and silently. Violence was deliberately directed against civilians and not against opposing forces, with the aim of establishing ethnically pure territories. Kaldor became convinced that outside forces were needed to protect ordinary people while Beebe and his fellow officers began to realize that the traditional heavy-military war-fighting machine was quite inappropriate for this kind of operation.

Following the war over Kosovo, Kaldor was a member of the Independent International Commission on Kosovo, chaired by the distinguished South African judge, Richard Goldstone. Beebe was deployed in the province. Kaldor favored military intervention to prevent the ethnic cleansing of Kosovar Albanians by Serb forces but was dismayed by the method chosen—aerial bombing. You cannot help killing civilians when bombs are dropped from 15,000 feet even though it is called "collateral damage," and Milosevic, the president of Serbia, was able to use the bombing by NATO forces as a cover to speed up ethnic cleansing. NATO prevailed in the end, and the Kosovar Albanians returned to Kosovo—but after much trauma. Many Serbs were then expelled in revenge, leaving the province as divided as ever. As the U.S. Army attaché focusing on security needs in Kosovo after the war, Beebe found that his expertise was needed not to identify what kind of army Kosovo required but to advise on how to deal with unexploded ordnance, erratic water and electricity supplies, and lack of sanitation. Both Serbs and Albanians considered these issues security priorities.

The War on Terror provided yet another test of our thinking on security issues. The language of "security" became visible in daily newspaper headlines, and entire government departments claimed the term. Kaldor was asked by the European Union's (EU) foreign-policy chief, Javier Solana, to convene a study group to come up with some ideas about European security capabilities. They produced two reports—the Barcelona Report and the Madrid Report—both concluding that Europe needed not a conventional national security policy but to be able to contribute to human security.

For that, you need a combination of military and civilian capabilities, a set of principles about how they should be used, and a new legal framework. The study group realized that Europe needed to be able to help fill the "security gap." Millions of people in the world live in conditions of intolerable insecurity. They risk being killed, robbed, tortured, and/or raped; and they risk dying from disease or lack of food, clean water, and/or sanitation; they risk dying in storms, floods, and famines, which are increasingly common because of climate change.

Yet our security forces are designed to fight twentieth century wars. Europe has 1.8 million men and women under arms, but only a fraction of them can be deployed to areas of insecurity, where they find themselves inappropriately trained and equipped.

During the same period, as the senior Africa analyst for the U.S. Army, Beebe was asked to conduct a research project on how Africans understand security. From interviews with high-level ministers, defense personnel, NGO members, academics, and even four or five Somali cab drivers in Washington, D.C.—a fairly clear message emerged. They pointed to several items needed for African security: reform of the security sector, including law-and-order reform, police reform, judicial reform, penal-code and penal-system reform, and the transformation of standing military forces into a value-added instrument for social development.

That was somewhat familiar territory to Beebe. But then three issues emerged that were so far out of the U.S. Department of Defense's thinking that Beebe knew the Army couldn't help him. He'd have to look elsewhere for an answer to the threats posed by health, poverty, and climate change.

At this point our worlds converged. Beebe read the EU study-group reports and sent an e-mail to Kaldor, which began a discussion that led to this book. We have separately and together concluded that the world needs a paradigm shift in the way we think about security. We need an alternative to the concept of the "War on Terror." The state-based security architectures of the twentieth century cannot address twenty-first-century vulnerabilities. We need to make a core shift from focusing on traditional threats to focusing on conditions-based vulnerabilities. These vulnerabilities individually could never be seen as threats, but when blended together they create a very unstable reality.

Beebe pictures it like a house of cards: you don't know which card is going to be pulled out, but you can be sure that when that card is pulled out, the house will fall. You don't know how fast it will fall, whether it will fall entirely or partially, or in which direction the debris will spill—but you know that it will fall because our systems cannot absorb any kind of shock.

Security for this century is a concern of not only the departments of defense but also civilian agencies and NGOs. It's a multidimensional challenge. We cannot achieve something we have no words for, and we do not yet have the words to describe twenty-first-century security in a way that is agreeable to both militaries and the humanitarian community. With this book, we hope to begin to create a new language.

■

What do we mean by "human security"? First, human security is about the everyday security of individuals and the communities in which they live rather than the security of states and borders. It is about the security of *Angolans*, not the security of Angola.

Second, it is about different sorts of security, not just protection from the threat of foreign enemies. It is about not being killed or robbed or forcibly expelled from your home—the sort of insecurity experienced in violent upheavals such as those in Afghanistan or Cabinda. But it also includes not losing your home in a hurricane or a forest fire, having enough to eat and drink, and being able to go to a doctor if you are ill. It is about both freedom from fear and freedom from want. The two biggest attacks on the United States in the twenty-first century have been Hurricane Katrina and 9/11—neither was an attack by an enemy state.

Finally, human security recognizes the interrelatedness of security in different places. Violence and resentment, poverty and illness—in places such as Africa, Central Asia, or the Middle East—travel across the world through terrorism, transnational crime, or pandemics. Instead of allowing insecurity to travel, we need to send security in the opposite direction. The kind of security that Americans and Europeans expect to enjoy at home has to spread to the rest of the world. We can no longer keep our part of the world safe while ignoring other places. The world is interconnected through social media, transportation, and basic human sympathy.

The idea of human security was first put forward in the 1994 Human Development Report published by the United Nations Development Programme (UNDP). The report argued that the concept of security has "for too long been interpreted narrowly: as security of territory from external aggression, or as protection of national interests in foreign policy or as global security from a nuclear holocaust. It has been related more to nation states than to people."[1] The report identified seven core elements, which together made up the concept of human security—economic security, food security, health security, environmental security, personal security, community security, and political security.

At that time, the main concern was to make sure that the peace dividend expected from the end of the Cold War would be devoted to development. The aim of the 1994 Human Development Report was to use the concept of security to emphasize the urgency of development. This broad definition of human security was adopted by the Japanese government and taken up by the United Nations's High-Level Panel on Threats, Challenges and Change in their report, *In Larger Freedom*, and in the Secretary-General's response to that report.[2]

A narrower definition of the concept of human security, developed by the Canadian government, is closely associated with the concept of Responsibility to Protect—the idea that the international community has a responsibility to protect people threatened by genocide, ethnic cleansing, and other massive violations of human rights when their governments fail to act. This definition is reflected in the Human Security Report, published in 2005, and the subsequent Human Security Briefs, documents that provide valuable information about political violence—particularly violent conflicts.[3]

Our version of human security emphasizes what the UNDP calls personal security—the security of human beings in violent upheavals. Thus we agree with the idea of Responsibility to Protect. But we also think that it is impossible to protect people from violence without taking into account all of the other dimensions of insecurity—the conditions of violence. In the Report of the Commission on Human Security, the Nobel Prize–winning economist Amartya Sen focuses on what he calls the downside risks: "the insecurities that threaten human survival or the safety of daily life, or imperil the natural dignity of men and women, or expose human beings to the uncertainty of disease and pestilence, or subject vulnerable people to abrupt penury."[4]

A human-security approach aims, above all, to prevent violence by tackling the conditions that lead to violence. But where people are in the midst of violent upheavals, as is the case now in Afghanistan, it also focuses on how to dampen down the violence rather than on how to "win." And in the aftermath of violent upheavals, a human-security approach looks not just at reconstruction but also at preventing new outbreaks of violence, since the conditions that led to violence—weak rule of law, unemployment, criminality, surplus weapons, loss of livelihood, or extremist ideologies—are often worse after conflict than before.

So, are we arguing that armies should turn their swords into plowshares? No. There is an essential role for force in human-security operations: sometimes you need to be able to protect people using what is known as hard power. But militaries must work together with civilians—police officers, health workers, development experts, and others—and their role is very different from traditional war fighting. In the Barcelona and Madrid reports, the study group that Kaldor convened developed six principles of human security that apply to both military and civilians working together in zones of insecurity.

These are

1. **The Primacy of Human Rights**. In human-security operations, the goal is protecting civilians, not defeating an enemy.
   This means that human rights, including the rights to life, education, clean water, and housing—must be respected—even
   in the midst of conflict. If they are not, outside interventions
   can fuel insurgencies.
2. **Legitimate Political Authority.** In the long run, human security can only be provided by local authorities whom people
   trust. This might be a state, a municipality or a provincial administration. The job of outside forces is to create safe spaces
   where people can freely engage in a political process that can
   establish legitimate authorities.
3. **A Bottom-up Approach.** The population affected by violence
   and insecurity must be involved in a human-security strategy,
   and yet the international community often operates in protected enclaves without communicating with people. Ulti-
   mately, the people who live in areas of insecurity must solve
   their own problems. Outsiders can help but only if they understand what is needed; otherwise they risk making things
   worse.
4. **Effective Multilateralism.** If outsiders are to have the consent
   of the local population, they must be seen as legitimate, which
   means operating within the framework of international law,
   especially under a UN mandate. Security policies cannot be
   effective if they are spread out among many different agencies,
   governments, and NGOs.
5. **Regional Focus.** Human insecurity has no clear boundaries.
   It spreads through refugees, criminal and extremist networks,
   and through economic and environmental calamities. There
   are many 'bad neighbourhoods' in the world such as Central

Asia, the Horn of Africa, the Caucasus, and parts of the Middle East and Central Africa.

6. **Clear Civilian Command.** In human security operations, civilians are in command. This means that the military must operate in support of law and order and under rules of engagement that are more similar to those of police work than to the rules of armed combat. Everyone needs to know who is in charge, and leaders must be able to communicate politically with local people as well as people in the sending countries.

■

We are frequently asked how a human security paradigm applies to ongoing conflicts in Iraq and Afghanistan. In particular, how would a human security approach fit in the alternatives that are being proposed, at the time of writing, by the Obama Administration? The wars in Iraq and Afghanistan were conceived (in 2003 and 2001) as conventional military conflicts and they remain substantially affected by that initial conception. In both places, the level of violence, as we argue in Chapter 4, is much higher as a consequence of the way force was used in the early stages. It is very difficult, half way through an as yet incomplete war, to shift direction if for the previous several years you have been shooting at the people you are now offering to protect. It lacks credibility. Local populations are deeply sceptical of such claims—and with good reason.

So while the principles of Human Security are important in both countries, the application of them is hindered by the fact that conventional miltiary engagements have recently dominated in both places.

The human security that the book describes is aimed at helping to end conflict in Afghanistan and Iraq but, much more, at preventing the future misuse of ineffective twentieth century militarism without denying the fact that the world's democracies need to be engaged in the politically and economically needy insecure parts of the world. So, bearing that qualification in mind, what would a human security strategy for Afghanistan entail?

Human security is both an ends and a means. If a human security approach were to be adopted in Afghanistan, the goal would be the security of ordinary Afghans. At present, the goal of Western operations in Afghanistan is the defeat of what are seen as foreign enemies. As President Obama put it in his speech announcing the surge at West Point on December 1, 2009: "Our overarching goal remains the same: to disrupt, dismantle, and defeat Al-Qaeda in Afghanistan and Pakistan, and to prevent its capacity to threaten America and our allies in the future."[5]

Those who oppose the war in Afghanistan argue, with some justice, that far from defeating Al-Qaeda, the international presence in Afghanistan provokes new attacks. Al-Qaeda is one of those Hydra-headed phenomena that pop up in different places. The terrorists who attacked London in July 2005 were all British and all went to school in Huddersfield, Yorkshire, even though they later trained in Pakistan. The terrorist who nearly blew up a KLM plane travelling to Detroit on Christmas Day 2009 was a British educated Nigerian who trained in Yemen. The raison d'etre of Al-Qaeda is the war against the west, which they call jihad. The more Al-Qaeda is attacked, the more it attracts disenchanted and alienated young people. Every air strike, especially when civilians are killed, seems to offer evidence for a storyline in which to make sense of their frustrations.

A human security approach would favour the international presence in Afghanistan but not primarily to defeat Al-Qaeda rather to protect Afghans. Of course, the surge strategy emphasises the security of Afghans. In his surge speech, President Obama talked about bringing an end to the "era of war and suffering," but this is seen as a means to an end—the defeat of Al-Qaeda—rather than an end in itself. In a human security approach, it should be the other way round. It might be necessary to defeat Al-Qaeda in order to protect Afghans. The difference is not merely semantic. It matters in both political and practical terms. Afghans will never fully trust the outside presence as long as they fear that Afghan lives are secondary to the lives of internationals,. In practical terms, Afghan lives will be risked if the primary goal is to defeat Al-Qaeda. If attacking terrorists, with air strikes or drones or whatever, is considered necessary—even if it means risking the lives of Afghan civilians—then it will be very hard for Afghans to trust the international presence and it will be even harder to stabilise Afghanistan. The tension between the security of Afghans and the war against Al-Qaeda, the War on Terror in another guise, is the central contradiction of current operations.

Western policymakers and policy shapers argue that the Western public would never accept a rationale based on the security of Afghans rather than the threat of Al-Qaeda. Richard Holbrooke, the U.S. Special Representative to Afghanistan and Pakistan, insists that it is only because of the link between the Taliban and Al-Qaeda that the international presence is needed.

> "If the Taliban were just another awful odious social movement with terrible values, with certain points of view we don't agree with, it would be a serious problem, but it would not justify the commitment of what will ultimately be 100,000 American troops after this build-up is completed and a good number of our allied troops numbering in the 35 [thousand] to 45,000 range at least, including build-up and commitments still to come."[6]

Why, it is argued, should we protect Afghans and not, say Congolese or Somalis?

There are two answers to this question. One is that we have a special responsibility to Afghans because we invaded their country in 2001. Whatever the rightness or wrongness of that initial decision, we cannot now leave Afghans less secure and less free than they were in 2001. The other is that if we are to be secure, the world needs to be secure and we do, indeed, need to be able to help Congolese and Somalis along with others. In the long-term, this means a much greater global commitment to providing the resources – people, money, expertise—for human security. This may not mean a commitment on the scale of Iraq and Afghanistan simply because, as we elaborate in this book, the use of conventional military force in twenty-first century crises makes things much worse.

So if human security is the goal, what are the means? It would involve a big commitment of military and civilian personnel acting according to the principles of human security. Perhaps the biggest difference between a human security approach and a counter-insurgency approach is the first principle—primacy of *human rights*. Of course, the Taliban and Al-Qaeda are the main groups violating human rights. But other sources of human rights violations would have to be addressed and the Taliban is adept at exploiting those violations to mobilise support. Particularly important is collateral damage. Roughly the same number of civilians (slightly less) have been killed in air strikes as killed by the Taliban and Al-Qaeda. General McCrystal, the Commander in Afghanistan, has ordered troops not to pursue Taliban fighters at the risk of civilian casualties— nevertheless some 1013 civilians were killed in Afghanistan in the first half of 2009, at least half from American air strikes. Moreover there have been some 600 drone attacks against targets in Pakistan since President Obama took office.

There is a strange disconnect in thinking about attacks on Al-Qaeda. President Obama is very sensitive to the need to follow the precepts of human rights and 'just war' doctrine as he made clear in his speech accepting the Nobel Peace Prize. This is why he ordered an end to torture and the closing down of Guantanamo Bay. Yet drone attacks are also human rights violations. They would be unthinkable against home grown terrorists. Imagine if the British government had decided to attack Huddersfield in the aftermath of the 7/7 bombings. Of course we have to catch terrorists, but through intelligence and policing. Suspects need to be arrested not arbitrarily killed. Drone attacks exemplify the double standards about the lives of Afghans and Pakistanis compared to Americans or Europeans. The lyrics of a popular Pakistani song say the Americans regard Pakistanis as insects.

Other human rights violations experienced by Afghans include violations by the government, the police, and governors—who rule in a corrupt, repressive, predatory way within a weak rule of law and an absence or perversion of justice; domestic violence including widespread violations of women's rights; criminality, especially the drug trade, which now accounts for a large share of the total economy; unemployment; poverty; lack of access to healthcare and education; clean water and sanitation; and other violations of economic and social rights. These human rights violations need to receive as much attention as the threat from the Taliban insurgency.

There has been, at the time of writing, a lot of emphasis on the civilian surge—assistance in helping build up security forces, police and justice systems, and development aid—especially for agriculture as an alternative to the drug economy. But the numbers of civilians are tiny in comparison with the military effort and they are hampered by the dominance of the military.

The civilian effort depends on the establishment of humanitarian space—protected zones in which economic and social needs can be addressed and in which a political process free of fear can be initiated. But that is extremely difficult in the midst of a shooting war against the Taliban and Al-Qaeda, even though there are very important efforts going on now to help create protected communities along these lines.

The second principle is *legitimate political authority*. Perhaps the biggest obstacle to a human security approach at the moment is continued Western support to the Karzai government. The Hamid Karzai's administration includes many former commanders, often known as warlords, who violate human rights and are heavily engaged in the drug trade—and which just passed repressive legislation on women. In particular, the police, whom the West trains, are corrupt and predatory. The fraudulent elections in the autumn of 2009 may have made things worse, even though Western governments extracted promises from President Karzai to reform.

What is needed is much more emphasis on justice—the vetting of people in key positions like members of parliament, governors, police, and soldiers—and the reconstruction of governance at local levels. As McCrystal has said: "It is not about how many people you kill—it's about how many you convince."[7] As long as the government lacks legitimacy and indeed preys upon the population, Afghans may seek protection from the hated Taliban. Recent proposals to start a reconciliation process with the Taliban are seen by many Afghans as a way of making the government even less legitimate, creating an unholy alliance of warlords and the Taliban. They also fear that effort to attract low level fighters to the government side through inducements may merely result in increased recruitment to the Taliban.

To establish a legitimate political authority, the *bottom-up approach* is critical. Legitimacy is all about the relationship between the government and the people, and it is civil society that mediates this relationship. Unfortunately, most members of the international community that remain are confined to bases and travel around in protected convoys so they have little interaction with the population. A lot of emphasis is placed on cultural understanding and the assistance of anthropologists and other experts. But the real point is that Afghans are at least as sophisticated and self-reflective as Amer-

icans. The best way to understand what is going is to have long discussions with Afghans, not social scientists, although the latter can
help. The emphasis on culture is actually a bit patronising—
Afghans can understand different cultures, but there is such a thing
as basic human respect and politeness. A very important element
of the surge strategy is the injunction to 'Live alongside the population'; this is critical for developing a bottom-up approach at local
levels. But it is also important to engage with civil society in the
cities. It is often argued that the English-speaking intellectuals in
Kabul do not really understand what is going on in the countryside.
Actually, many civil society activists in cities do not speak English
and complain that internationals take their translators to talk to warlords but not to them. But whether or not they speak English, those
educated Afghans who organize NGOs and human rights groups
or who teach in schools and universities, know at least as much as
internationals and need to be much more involved in discussions
about strategy. It would be odd if governments in London or Washington ignored the policy communities in those cities on the
grounds that they are out of touch with the rest of the country.

Internationals tend to talk more to the warlords because they are
often the problem but, though this may be necessary, civic activists
can offer guidance on the best approach.

The third principle is *effective multilateralism*. At present, in
Afghanistan, there are two commands—the NATO command au-
thorised by the UN and the U.S. Command Operation Enduring
Freedom. Even though McCrystal has taken command of both, in
effect these two commands epitomize the tension between human
security and the War on Terror. There should be a single UN command, explicitly aimed at the protection of Afghans.

In addition, in Afghanistan there are huge numbers of different
agencies, governments, NGOs etc, very badly coordinated and all
absorbing the aid effort that is supposed to be for Afghans. There

needs to be better coordination, fewer separate agencies, and a common coherent strategy. Indeed, this is one of the arguments for a human security approach. It is very difficult to achieve institutional coherence when every new mechanism created to coordinate the institutions tends to add another bureaucratic layer. But human security could provide the basis for conceptual coherence — something that is impossible at the moment because not all of the agencies and NGOs accept the American rationale.

The need for *regional focus*, the fifth principle, is obvious. The "new war" in Afghanistan extends over borders, especially into Pakistan. Indeed, the terrorist attacks on Mumbai in November 2008 exposed the regional ramifications of the violence. The drug routes and human trafficking routes go through Iran and Uzbekistan. And Russia and China are needed to help with alternative supply routes. This is why Afghanistan's neighbours have to be involved in a common strategy. There should be regional talks at all levels of government and civil society.

The final principle is *clear civilian command*. Counter-insurgency is a military strategy. A human security approach needs to be led by a powerful civilian — the UN Special representative or Richard Holbrooke as the U.S. Special Representative. Even though Richard Holbrooke is supposed to be the civilian counterpart to General Petraeus, he is much less visible both in the region and internationally. The military need to be thought of as contributing to a civilian strategy rather than the other way round. Civilian control is necessary if the needs of people are to be put at the top of the agenda in practice as well as in theory. Civilian control would have to mean different rules of engagement, based on human rights rather the "laws of war." It would also create more space for economic, social and political development.

The surge strategy undoubtedly moves in the direction of these principles. But they are hampered both by the strategic narrative –

the emphasis on the defeat of Al-Qaeda—and by the fact that they are militarily led. The McCrystal strategy should have been the Holbrooke strategy. There needs to be a public face to the international effort—a person who communicates with Afghans as well as the international community and who is not seen as a war leader.

The argument for a human security approach is not an argument against addressing the problem of terrorism. On the contrary, the terrorist threat is so serious we cannot afford to elevate the status of Al-Qaeda by treating them as traditional enemies. Rather than being defeated or killed, they have to be isolated, marginalised and arrested. That is how criminals are dealt with in societies that take human security for granted such as the United States or Britain.

■

If ours is *an era of persistent conflict,* as the United States Army Chief of Staff has said, then we must change our thinking, change the paradigm, and change the language. This book is a kind of manual for human security and, at the same time, it is a learning process. It is not intended to blame any one political grouping or philosophy, but rather to challenge twentieth century conventional wisdom and to start a discussion about a new language that is relevant to all people in the twenty-first century. This new language is as important for the government, academia, NGOs, and the general public as it is for the military. It is a 360 degree shift in security thinking.

This book journeys through various regional conflicts and tries to show the limitations of twentieth century approaches to the kinds of security challenges that we believe will characterize the current era. It also tries to describe what an alternative approach might look like.

We conclude by reflecting on our title: "The Ultimate Weapon." The ultimate weapon in the twenty-first century simply cannot be something like the F-22 combat aircraft—not even something conceptually close to it. Indeed, we argue that in some circumstances the F-22 is almost as damaging to its user as it is to its targets. Finding the ultimate weapon requires a radical change of mindset. Even though most of us believe in human equality in the abstract, in practice, we do not act as though Afghan or African lives are equal to American and British lives. But they are, and that is where human security begins.

2

The Twenty-First Century Risks

The twenty-first century began when the Cold War ended. During the Cold War, we believed that a third world war, a nuclear holocaust, was the worst possible threat to human security. While the use of nuclear weapons is an ever-present possibility, our more immediate concern is a much more complicated mix of political violence, crime, material deprivation, and environmental degradation. Twentieth-century militaries were developed to defeat the ground forces, air forces, and naval forces of an enemy state. The threats of the twenty-first century will more closely resemble forces of nature. The instruments of security developed in the Cold War are increasingly unsuited for managing this.

In this chapter, we tell the stories of Sarajevo and Goma, two cities that typify the kind of human insecurity experienced in many parts of the world in the twenty-first century.

■

Returning to Sarajevo in July 1993 in the middle of the war, on a mission to support the Helsinki Citizens' Assembly, Mary Kaldor was greeted by Haris Pasovic, the theater director. "Welcome to the twenty-first century," he said. "Come and see the beginning of the end of Western civilization." At that time, what the Bosnians called the "multi-multi spirit" (multiethnic, multicultural, and multireligious) of Sarejevo was being strenuously preserved. Mixed marriages and mutual celebrations of festivals were still taking place. More importantly, the city was determined to remain secular, irreverent, cultured, and as Sarajevans liked to say, "European." Because the airport was being shelled, Kaldor got stuck in Sarajevo. She spent her time doing what Sarajevans did: going to concerts and art exhibitions and, of course, to the theater. She watched a naughty English comedy performed by candlelight. It was called *How to Get Rid of Your Wife*, and the audience rocked with laughter as wives, prostitutes, men dressed up as women, and policemen frolicked about on the darkened stage—drowning out the sound of shelling outside. "What's it got to do with Sarajevo?" someone asked the director afterwards. "Everything," he said. "It's funny."

All this took place against the backdrop of war. The week before Kaldor's visit, some thirty-one people had been killed and 194 wounded. Since the siege of Sarajevo, which began in 1992, 8,871 people had been killed, including 1,401 children, and 16,660 people wounded. On the streets you could be hit by sniper fire from Serbs encamped in the hills around Sarajevo. Shelling was continuous—it felt like a permanent thunderstorm. Locals learned where to take cover and how to cross the more exposed roads—the road from the airport, for instance, was known as Snipers' Alley. You could easily get picked up by one of the more fearsome Bosnian commanders and find yourself forced to dig trenches while exposed to Serbian fire. There were some thirty-six groups who called themselves armies (militias, criminal gangs, self-defense groups) in Sarajevo alone. Crime was rife.

Imports were blocked by the siege—except what came through the United Nations High Commission for Refugees (UNHCR) by air, which was totally inadequate. The monthly rations, which arrived by the same plane as Kaldor, included, for each family: one kilo of flour, half a kilo of rice, half a liter of oil, one tin of beef, three soaps, and a packet of biscuits for people over sixty. The black market flourished; a lot could be bought with foreign currencies or cigarettes. People were exhausting their life savings.

As one person put it, living in Sarajevo was like a very expensive foreign holiday. There was no water or electricity; gas was supplied intermittently, when permitted by the Serbs. Most of the trees in Sarajevo had been cut down for fuel. A colleague of Kaldor's, Zdravko Grebo, a professor of international law at the University of Sarajevo and chair of the Yugoslav branch of the Helsinki Citizens' Assembly, showed her how to soak the pages of books in water and roll them out when dry to make fuel for cooking. The works of Lenin, he told her, made particularly good fuel.

The people of Sarajevo were trying to preserve the city's multi-multi character while it was being attacked by Serb nationalists. Both Serb and Croat nationalists wanted to carve out ethnically pure territories. The technique of the nationalists was ethnic cleansing. The Serbs, for example, would start by shelling a village and terrifying the local inhabitants. They would then send in a paramilitary group with lists of rich Muslims or Croats as well as intellectuals, who would be killed and their homes looted. They would separate men and women. Men were often detained in detention camps; women were raped and expelled. Historic buildings and cultural symbols were destroyed. The long-preserved footprint of Gavrilo Princip, when he assassinated Archduke Ferdinand, sparking the First World War, was concreted over by Muslim nationalists because Princip was a Serb. The beautiful national library of Sarajevo, a unique example of Ottoman and Austro-Hungarian architecture, was shelled; all of its irreplaceable manuscripts in Persian, Arabic, Latin, and all of the Yugoslav languages—which documented the "multi-multi" history of Bosnia and Herzegovina as well as Yugoslavia—went up in flames. The shreds of burned manuscripts that floated around Sarajevo were known as "black butterflies."

Sarajevo during the siege was full of foreigners. United Nations peacekeeping troops were supposed to be delivering humanitarian assistance. International agencies like UNHCR and the International Committee of the Red Cross were represented. There were international NGOs and solidarity groups like the women's groups who delivered humanitarian aid in vans called Faith and Hysteria. The Montpelier branch of the Helsinki Citizens' Assembly had established an office in Sarajevo. There were foreign mercenaries who helped to train and equip the thirty-six armies. And, of course, there were many journalists. The foreigners were, by and large, protected from the war. They wore flak jackets and helmets to protect themselves from snipers. They had special blue passes that allowed them to cross checkpoints and move from Serb-controlled zones to Bosnian or Croat zones and back again. Many of them lived in the Holiday Inn, where they paid in foreign currency and were able to take baths or showers and eat proper food. Early in the morning, American journalists could be seen jogging along the corridors before their morning trips to report on what was happening. When they all returned after curfew at ten o'clock, dinner was served in the dining room, which was full of well-known people, like Christiane Amanpour and David Rieff, and abuzz with card games and discussions of the latest news. They all lived in a wildly different, and much healthier, reality than the Sarajevans.

Yet all of these foreigners seemed powerless to stop the war. Kaldor met General Morillon, the commander of the UN troops (who had his own chef flown out from France). He told her that he had developed plans to lift the siege of Sarajevo and that he thought it was feasible with the troops currently in Sarajevo. He also asserted that he had the mandate to lift the siege; United Nations Security Council Resolution 770 authorized UN troops to use "all necessary means" to ensure the supply of humanitarian assistance to the civilian population of Bosnia and Herzegovina. This was what is known as a Chapter VII operation, which allows UN troops to use force even without the consent of local parties. But not until the very end of the war was the order given to lift the siege.

The Helsinki Citizens' Assembly and other groups issued a long stream of proposals to the international community. They called for an international protectorate for Bosnia and Herzegovina. They called for safe havens, for lifting the siege of Sarajevo, for war-crime trials, and for protection of the civilian population from ethnic cleansing. Yet although some of these proposals were adopted, they were never fully backed and implemented. Not nearly enough troops were sent to defend the safe havens, and although the mandate was strong on paper, they never received the orders that would have allowed them to defend the safe havens. Moreover, peace proposals never got as much press coverage as violence. Kaldor, Zdravko Grebo, and Haris Pasovic held a press conference in the Holiday Inn to issue what they called the "Last-Chance Appeal for Sarajevo," but only two journalists came. The main effort of the international community was talks with the warring parties — the very people who were committing heinous war crimes.

The war finally ended when ethnic cleansing was complete. At least 100,000 people[1] were killed and more than two-thirds of the population expelled from their homes. It is true that Western aircraft shelled Serb positions at the very end of the war and that British and French ground troops lifted the siege of Sarajevo. But basically, the international community, through talks and in the Dayton Peace Accords, legalized what had happened on the ground: the partitioning of Bosnia into separate Serb, Muslim, and Croat parts. A substantial

international presence remains in the country to sustain that agreement and to prevent the few remaining flashpoints (Sarajevo, Brcko,
and Mostar) from flaring up again. A hugely complicated and dysfunctional state apparatus provides jobs for the extremist parties and
presides over a largely illicit economy in which unemployment is
very high and crime is rampant. The "multi-multi" spirit has largely
ebbed. Many young people want to leave. Sarajevo, by any reckon-
ing, is hardly "secure."

■

A decade later, Shannon Beebe visited Goma in Eastern Congo,
on a mission to assess the environmental impact of conflict. He flew
there from Kinshasa, the capital of Democratic Republic of the
Congo, on a flight with the UN Organization Mission in DR Congo
(MONUC), provided by the workhorse aviation NGO Air Serv International. MONUC is one of the largest UN missions in the
world. Beebe had been told that this flight was the only reliable connection between Kinshasa and the eastern provinces. Indeed, just
a few days before, a passenger airliner from Goma had crashed after
it struck lava at the end of the runway and then cut a swath through
Goma until the wreckage came to rest in the downtown area. The
U.S. embassy had banned all flights except Air Serv's MONUC
shuttle flights.

The flight to Goma was magnificent, crossing over the expanse
of the DRC and the lush jungle below. As the plane began its final
approach into Goma a sprinkling of colored canopies started to appear in the jungle. As the plane got closer to the ground, Beebe no-
ticed that these canopies were makeshift living quarters.

The ride from the airport to the heart of Goma was surrounded
by a press of humanity. People were carrying anything and everything, by all possible means and methods along, roads that were pit-

ted and pocked enough to rake out the transmission from almost
any vehicle. Driving was painstakingly slow. The only things that
seemed to be perfectly at home in these conditions were the many
Chinese-made motor scooters weaving in and out of traffic, people,
animals, and whatever other obstacles appeared.

Beebe's driver pointed out where the airliner crash had happened. He reported that since there were no fire brigades, people
had formed a human chain and put out the fires by handing cups
of water in assembly-line fashion. Once the fires had burned out
everything had been scavenged, including the sheet metal from the
aircraft. The only things left were too heavy to lift.

Eastern Congo saw the brunt of what was known as "Africa's
World War" during the late 1990s. During Beebe's visit it still suffered from the ravages of conflict between four rebel groups struggling for preeminence in various resource-rich areas. The
population lived in a constant state of fear. Some estimates put the
number of war dead in the Congo as high as 5 million.

This area is home to tin, coltan, cassiterite, and diamond mines.
The potential Gross Domestic Product (GDP) of this region is staggering, yet instability made wealth possible for only a few political
and economic predators with ties to the "democratic" government in
Kinshasa, 1,000 miles away. The area was wracked by uncertainty.
Politically motivated killings were commonplace; mass rapes and
atrocities occurred almost daily. Despite the Lusaka Ceasefire Agreement signed in 1999, which established the MONUC mission, violence has continued unabated in eastern Congo.

Beebe eventually arrived at his hotel on the outskirts of town. It
was beautifully situated on a peninsula jutting into Lake Kivu. As
the driver pulled up to two heavy iron gates, he sounded the horn
and then waited. A few moments later, there was movement behind
the gate and a small slit opened; two eyes peered through. Beebe
asked the driver why such security was necessary so far out of

town—was the place robbed or looted a lot? The driver responded, "It's complicated."

The owners of the hotel were of Tutsi origin, and just last week the owner's brother had been killed. The entire family suspected that the killers were a government "hit squad" who saw the family as threats to the government—the family had money and were Tutsi. Anyone with influence in the area, not directly associated with the central government of Kinshasa, was perceived as opposition and as a threat. Inside the gates, the Karibu Resort looked like a paradise. It was pristine. Everything was perfectly manicured and cared for. The only thing that seemed a bit peculiar was that there was only one other car.

The primary focus of Beebe's trip was to go to Virunga National Park to learn more about the illegal charcoal trade endangering the oldest national park in Africa and the killing of six Mountain Gorillas just a few months before. Sentries of the Congolese army were posted almost every other kilometer on the road leading out of Goma to the park. The soldiers lived in lean-tos or poncho liners stretched out with a pot underneath. Beebe asked the driver how long they stayed in those conditions, and he shook his head, not really wanting to discuss it. "I don't know. Maybe a few weeks. Maybe a couple of months." Beebe thought he didn't understand the question and asked specifically how long the soldiers lived in these locations without relief. He shook his head again, answering, "Yes, yes. I understand. They live there. Where else will they go?"

They continued on up the road for a few hours, finally reaching the ranger station—a beautiful building constructed in the early 1920s that must have been magnificent in its heyday. Now, there was no electricity, heat, or running water of any kind. Beebe and his companion were greeted by a host of curious park rangers. The interim director of the park asked if Beebe was there to do a story on the gorilla killings. Beebe said he wasn't, but was instead trying

to understand how the conflict was impacting the natural environment and people there and vice versa. The director smiled wryly
and asked, "So you are actually interested in the people of Kivu?
That's different."

The story he told was heartbreaking. The instability in the region
had driven many rebel groups to look for income from the charcoal
trade, which in North Kivu was worth nearly $30 million per year,
while locals' average salary was around $7 per month. All groups
were involved in some way with charcoaling. The groups soon realized that some of the largest and best trees were in Virunga National Park. Beebe asked if they didn't understand that there was far
more revenue to be gained by ecotourism lured in by the presence
of mountain gorillas than by charcoaling, with its short-term and
finite potential for gain. The interim director looked at Beebe: "People are starving today. Why should they worry about something to-
morrow that may never happen?" It brought home the fact that
societies in conflict and in desperation will mortgage their futures
simply to survive today.

The rest of the story was horrible and sad. The gorilla family
had been executed because of the charcoal trade. The director of
Virunga National Park had been attempting to stop the charcoal-
making operations. Little did he know, the director of the North
Kivu province was receiving money from the trade and wanted
him fired in order to continue the operation. The regional director
hired one of the park rangers to assassinate the family of gorillas
to make the park director look incompetent—it would be passed
off as a "rebel attack" on the animals. No one knows for sure how
much the park ranger was paid, but most people think he was
hired for $25.

Beebe spent most of the rest of the day speaking with the rangers
and their families. Many of them had been brought up as sons of
rangers, grandsons of rangers and/or nephews of rangers. Their hearts

and souls were devoted to the park and its animals. Beebe asked many of the rangers if the government was regular about paying wages. "It's complicated," and a smile, was the usual response. Beebe found out that most of the rangers had not been paid in three months; they were barely subsisting. No wonder it had been so easy to corrupt one of their number.

After spending the day in Rutshuru, Beebe returned to Goma around 11 p.m. The streets were eerily silent compared to the nights before. Beebe knew something was amiss. He asked the driver what was going on, and he shook his head, saying, "I'm not sure, but it's not good." They arrived at the hotel and the normally chatty driver left promptly, saying only, "Have a good night, sir. Stay inside." The entire front desk was abandoned.

At 2:38 a.m. Beebe awoke to a sound he knew all too well. There are only a few things in the world that sound like AK-47 gunfire. In North Kivu at 2:38 in the morning there is only one thing that sounds like AK-47 gunfire. A fierce fight had broken out not more than 100 meters away. It ended suddenly. Once the sun came up, Beebe ventured outside.

When Beebe went to check out, the hotel owner's daughter, whom he'd never met before, was at the desk. She was visibly shaking and talking rapidly on a mobile. She was interrupted twice by employees coming up to tell her something. When she finally turned to Beebe, he asked her what had happened.

"A government assassination squad from Kinshasa was sent out here to murder my father, and they attacked our house last night," she said. The family had fled a few days before to Rwanda. Against her family's wishes, she had heard of the attack and crossed back over to see what had happened. "My family has owned this land and this hotel since the early 1970s. We are business people and want nothing more than stability for this area so we can have better business. This is our country too. Why does disagreement mean death?"

Beebe asked her if she thought it was because they were ethnic Tutsis. Her answer was telling: "I don't know what the reason is, but I do know we will get rebel protection now. What other choices do we have?"

Beebe nodded, "Yes, it's complicated."

■

Sarajevo and Goma represent the tragic underside of what we call globalization. Sarajevo was a middle-income city in Europe. Goma is a potentially rich city in Africa. Yet both have been engulfed by the typical twenty-first-century pattern of violence. Both cities are located in formerly authoritarian states that were massively weakened by opening up to the world. Yugoslavia was communist, even if its form of communism was mild by Soviet standards. The Congo had experienced periodic conflict since independence and had been ruled by a mad, brutal military dictator, Mobutu Sese Seko, who had siphoned away much wealth.

The term *globalization* is a catchall to refer to new features of the twenty-first century. It has something do with increased information, communication, and travel. It has something to do with the interconnectedness of people in different countries, organizations, and businesses. And it sometimes just means a global market, freer trade, and more foreign investment. But specifically what does globalization mean for places like Sarajevo or Goma?

In social and economic terms, globalization means a shift from place-based, often state-dominated sectors like agriculture and industry to a "weightless economy" centered on sectors like finance, design, or marketing, as well as myriad services (both formal and informal). The rise of the weightless economy has also meant the rise of a global middle class that speaks one of the world languages, communicates through the Internet and mobile phones, travels by air, and watches various world TV channels. In places like China and India, millions have been pulled out of poverty by success in the global market.

But at the same time, millions have been thrown out of work by a combination of state mismanagement and competition from the global market. Yugoslavia, for example, began its economic opening to the outside world in the early 1980s when it turned to the International Monetary Fund (IMF) for financial assistance. While the middle classes in places like Sarajevo could travel and speak English, many rural workers who owned small plots in the countryside and came to work in state-owned factories lost their jobs. It was young men of this type who formed the backbone of the nationalist militias and who resented the cosmopolitans in the towns.[2] The unscrupulous entrepreneurs of violence who manipulated this situation were often engaged in large-scale corruption and crime at the interstices of the state-controlled economy. One of the big figures of the Belgrade underground, whose militia, the "Tigers," carried out some of the worst atrocities, was known as Arkan; he owned a string of pizza parlors that were covers for the drug trade. The war dramatically accelerated these developments. In Bosnia and Herzegovina, industrial production was more or less wiped out and national income fell by 90 percent while crime flourished. Looting, pillaging, smuggling of cigarettes and alcohol, extraction of remittances from abroad through restriction of necessities at checkpoints, and "taxation" of humanitarian aid all became essential elements of the war economy. Even though there has been economic growth since the war's end, local and transnational crime and joblessness are still very high.

In DRC, or Zaire, as it was known between 1971 and 1997, the formal economy fell precipitously at the turn of the twenty-first century. Gross Domestic Product per capita fell from $380 in 1985 to $224 in 1990 to $85 ($0.23 a day) in 2000, making it one of the poorest countries in the world.[3] The formal economy basically collapsed through a combination of pervasive corruption and the inability to compete in world markets for basic commodities even before the war compounded these ills, engulfing the country in hyperinflation, epidemics such as HIV/AIDS, and unthinkable levels of impoverishment. An Amnesty International report details the ways in which the war provided opportunities to make money via activities such as looting (which was often accompanied by torture, killing, and/or rape), targeting harvests, stealing from medical centers, attacking and robbing villages, systematically pillaging food aid, and sexual exploitation.[4] Particularly important was the competition to control mineral wealth, including water, diamonds, coltan, cassiterite, tin, copper, timber, and, as Beebe found, charcoal. There is a growing demand for coltan for use in computers and mobile phones.

Although GDP per capita has recovered since the international effort, as happens in many post-conflict situations, human-development indicators such as life expectancy, literacy, and access to water and clean sanitation have continued to fall. In 2009, the DRC ranked 176th out of 182 in the UN's Human Development Report.[5]

There is a growing gap between ordinary people in DRC and a new global middle class, partly created by the international effort. Beebe saw this gap clearly when returning to Kinshasa to stay in the Grand Hotel. He might have been anywhere in the world. There were numerous shops, boutiques, and restaurants filled with goods from Europe, telephone cards, and CDs. In the restaurants sat large Congolese men surrounded by bodyguards. A few of them sat alone with just their protection squads standing watch, talking rapidly and animately on their mobile phones while others enjoyed the company of very attractive young women. In a country where over half the population lives on less than $1 per day, Beebe found that the simple task of checking e-mail in the hotel's business center cost $20—almost a month's wages for a local.

Up to now, the growth of the global market has been based on twentieth-century technology, particularly the use of fossil fuels. This has led to global warming, the loss of biological diversity, deforestation, pollution, shortages of resources, and the advent of environmental refugees. In both Sarajevo and Goma, the cutting down of trees for immediate survival imperils the long-term future of the planet. Twenty-first-century technologies offer more of the same but also the possibility of conservation and environmental protection.

Globalization has also wrought a profound cultural and ideological transformation. States like Yugoslavia and DRC lost their information monopolies. They could not sustain communism (in Yugoslavia) or postcolonial nationalism (in Congo). On the one hand, global communications have made possible much greater awareness of our shared human fate, of human-rights abuses in different parts of the world, and of the interdependence of the environment, health, and energy. On the other hand, local radio and television broadcasts in local languages, videos, and mobile phones reach people who do not have the reading habit and make possible mobilization of insecurity around various exclusive ideologies. The war in DRC was a spillover from the genocide in Rwanda, when hundreds of thousands of Tutsis were killed by the Hutu regime. There, the regime used the radio stations *Radio Rwanda* and *Radio Télévision Libre des Mille Collines* (RTLM) to mobilize ordinary Hutus to join the government-organized militias in a killing spree. In the former Yugoslavia, television was in the hands of different national republics. In the years leading up to the wars, a war in the imagination was already being conducted on television; people got swept up in historical narratives that shaped their understandings of the current conflict. Serbian television, for example, interspersed current events with stories about the Battle of Kosovo Polje in 1389 (when Ottoman Turkey defeated Serbia) and World War II (when a fascist Croatian regime killed Serbs along with Jews and Roma in concentration camps). As David Rieff reported in his gripping account of the war in Bosnia, young men in the hills above Sarajevo saw themselves as "ridding Europe of the Turks."[6]

In both Africa and the Balkans, stories circulated through Web sites, mobile phones, and videos—mobilizing sentiment among diasporas in other countries. In the Bosnian war, Croatian "weekend fighters" would come from Germany, where they worked, to join in what appeared like a fictional adventure.

In political terms, the formal political world has become more multipolar and multilateral under globalization. Global politics involving new multilateral institutions, states, emerging powers, and a range of non-state actors including international NGOs and global social movements is increasingly supplanting international relations, the world of strategy, and state-to-state diplomacy.

All states have to engage in a multilateral process. States remain the repositories of sovereignty and the key members of the multilateral system, but they no longer have the same hegemony of action or decision on the world stage.

For example, the global effort to stem climate change—the Kyoto Protocol—was formally negotiated among 170 countries. International agencies like the United Nations Environmental Programme (UNEP), the United Nations Development Programme (UNDP), and the World Meteorological Organization (WMO) also took part in the negotiations. Some 250 NGOs, including both businesses and environmental groups, as well as local authorities, observed the negotiations and lobbied governments—some of the environmental NGO's were organized into the Climate Action network.[7] The International Criminal Court (ICC) was an initiative of ten to fifteen "like-minded" countries, but the negotiations also involved a powerful network of NGOs—the Coalition for the International Criminal Court—and were hosted and promoted by the United Nations.[8]

These changes have created a hugely contradictory situation. Important decisions are made at a global level, but the basis of politics, particularly democratic politics, is still national. On the one hand, global communications makes it difficult for states to maintain information monopolies, and more and more people are demanding democracy. On the other, often states cannot respond to democratic demands because they are dependent on multinational corporations, international financial institutions like the IMF, or multilateral processes like the Kyoto Protocol or the ICC.

Indeed some states, caught between domestic struggles and outside pressures, have not been able to manage the transition to a more multilateral world. The domestic consensus that underpinned their rule has disappeared. They have been undermined by falling revenue—formal economies have declined; external aid has decreased (especially since the loss of superpower patrons at the end of the Cold War), and rapacious government officials have stolen significant amounts of the remaining funds. These states have lost legitimacy; their ruling ideologies appear increasingly hollow and they are less and less able to provide services or maintain infrastructure. They have been pulled apart by ethnic, religious, and tribal claims.

Perhaps the most important aspect of state weakness has been the loss of the monopoly on violence. For some countries, as in Europe, this is a result of transnationalization. Armed forces are integrated into multilateral security arrangements like NATO, and a range of international treaties has led to more and more arrangements for mutual exercises and inspections. But this is also a result of the privatization of violence.

Military technology has become more accurate and lethal. That is one reason twentieth century wars, in which armed forces fight

each other on the battlefield, have become so rare. Clashes between symmetrical opponents would lead to immensely destructive
stalemates, as in the Iran-Iraq war. At the same time, simple, light,
easy-to-use weapons can be acquired by non-state actors, even children, and used against unprotected targets. Authoritarian states
tend to proliferate security services so as to play them against each
other. As states can no longer afford high levels of military spending
nor the cost of maintaining law and order, bits of the insecurity
services break off; redundant or unpaid soldiers sell their services
and their weapons to all sorts of political and criminal groups.
Hence the spread of asymmetric violence, where civilians and population centers are leveraged as part of the warfare and crime.

In Yugoslavia, for example, territorial defense units (TOs) were
introduced in the 1970s after the Soviet invasion of Czechoslovakia.
They were trained and equipped for guerrilla warfare in the event
of a Soviet invasion. Yugoslavs participated in the military effort and
often owned their own weapons. As Serbia started to use the Yugoslav National Army, the separate republics started to arm the TOs
and the police with surplus weapons acquired from Eastern Europe
after the end of the Cold War. All sides started to recruit paramilitary and other armed groups. Foreign mercenaries were also involved; redundant British, French, and Italian soldiers helped to
train many of the gangs, while mujahideen from the Soviet war in
Afghanistan came to "help" the Muslims in Bosnia and Herzegovina. (Some of them married locals and stayed.)

Under Mobutu, Congolese unpaid soldiers were encouraged to
loot and pillage. Mobutu made desperate attempts to hold on to
power by creating more and more security services. In addition to
the army, there were border guards, a presidential guard, a gendarmerie, and various types of internal security forces. In the end,
Mobutu could only rely on his personal guard to protect him.
Meanwhile, the security forces that were no longer paid formed

their own paramilitary groups, all of which had easy access to weapons—both Cold War surplus and the CIA's use of the Congo as a conduit to supply weapons to Angolan rebels offered steady streams of arms through DRC.

Organizational forms have also changed in the global era. In place of the centralized, vertical, and hierarchical organizations of the twentieth century (e.g., militaries) are loose horizontal networks that link groups at all levels of society. Robert Reich likens the organizational structures of big corporations to spider webs; the proud names of companies have become brands or fronts for a complex mix of partnerships and subcontracts. Others talk of the "hollow" corporation, a description that also applies to politics—to governments, whose ministers are increasingly brokers of domestic interests and international agreements; to civil society, with its networks and coalitions of NGOs, social movements, and civic institutions like churches and universities; and to entrepreneurs of violence, who can now rally forces from global networks of disenfranchisement and despair. In Yugoslavia, the strategy of ethnic cleansing was carried out by networks of paramilitary groups and regular forces—that is, the Serbian army, which succeeded the Yugoslav National Army and the republican TOs. In DRC, the rebels under Laurent Nkunda were Congolese soldiers, Congolese Tutsi Banyamulenge, as well as Rwandan, Ugandan, and some Burundian government troops. The government side was also backed by the armed forces of neighboring states, including Angola, Zimbabwe, and Namibia. All sides mainly attacked civilian areas rather than each other.

So globalization has its good and bad sides. It has led to dramatic economic growth; it has increased our awareness that we live on a shared planet and are part of a single human community; it has spread openness and democracy; more and more states cooperate and are part of multilateral arrangements; organizations are less top-down and hierarchical; and there is more scope for individuals. But these changes have also created the dark underbelly of globalization—the combination of deprivation, exclusive ideologies, environmental and economic vulnerabilities, crime, and weak states that has given rise to networks of desperation (what are often described as creeping vulnerabilities or asymmetric risks or threats).

In violent upheavals, all the conditions that led to violence are made worse. The formal economy collapses and the state becomes even weaker. Young men often have little choice but to join the fighting or a criminal group. The war produces fear and hatred among ethnic or religious groups and thus helps to underpin exclusive ideologies. The need to finance the war further spreads criminality, which in turn further weakens the rule of law. This is why contemporary conflicts are so difficult to end; they strengthen the vested political and economic interests in war and create a vortex of violence. The warring parties need the war to mobilize extremist ideologies and to carry on the criminal activities (looting; pillaging; smuggling; trading in drugs, people, or valuables) through which the war is financed. Hence terms like *persistent*, *unending*, or *forever wars*.

New wars are not only difficult to contain in time; they are also difficult to contain in space. They spread through refugees and displaced persons; through transnational criminal activities; and through polarizing activities. They are the epicenter of "bad neighbourhoods" like the Horn of Africa, the Upper Nile, the Middle East, the Caucasus, and Central Asia.

There are international efforts to address these new phenomena. In both Yugoslavia and DRC there were peacekeeping troops. But although they were mandated to protect civilians, both the UN Protection Force in Yugoslavia (UNPROFOR) and the UN Organization Mission in DR Congo (MONUC) saw their tasks in military terms: to separate the opposing sides in the conflicts. These forces do not have enough troops and are not trained and equipped for this kind of task. They remain caught in twentieth-century military thinking in which soldiers are used to fight on one side or the other or to separate warring parties after a cease-fire. There is no doubt that the United Nations has been through a learning process over the past decade. UN forces have gotten better at helping to negotiate and sustain cease-fires, but they have not yet succeeded in providing human security.

Globalization does offer the possibility of a more cooperative world based on the idea of a single human community and the extension of law and politics across borders, but despite the growth of multilateralism there are mammoth obstacles in constructing such a world—obstacles that have to do with the national basis of politics and the difficulty of reorienting economic and environmental priorities. Not least is the difficulty of reorienting the way we think about security.

Twentieth-century solutions—for example, the use of military forces to fight wars in fragile situations—make things even worse. Twentieth-century military forces that once *produced* security may well be responsible for *consuming* security in the twenty-first century. If we maintain traditional ways of thinking along parochial institutional lines we will tend to destabilize rather than reinforce fragile systems. The use of military force to attack a house of cards can have catastrophic consequences. This is what happened after President George W. Bush announced the War on Terror.

3

The Twentieth-Century Mindset

The American victory in 1945 was perhaps the most glittering moment in American history. The Nazi threat had been defeated and democracy had been restored or established in Western Europe and Japan. Americans had been mobilized in the war effort, churning out more tanks, aircraft, and weapons than all American allies and enemies combined. The war was a triumph for American science and technology—in particular, for the new technique of mass production tied to the use of oil, the use of airpower, and the invention and first use of nuclear weapons. By the end of the war, the specter of unemployment seemed to have vanished and Gross National Product had leapt by 63 percent. Although nearly half a million American soldiers were killed in the war, the continental United States remained untouched.

Every American leader after the war felt compelled to remind the American public of that glittering moment. The story of America's moral crusade for freedom, supported by American technological know-how, has become the dominant narrative of the American state. The Cold War between the West and Communism that followed World War II froze that glittering moment. It was based on the same ideas: that America was ready to go to war to fight for freedom using all of the massive technological and industrial capabilities at its disposal and that war consisted of battles between armed forces in which the aim is total destruction of the enemy. Huge armies faced each other across the Fulda Gap in Germany for forty years, in readiness for World War III. Tens of thousands of long-range missiles and other high-tech weapons were permanently mobilized for potential use. Many of the same corporate giants that were so important in World War II developed and produced new generations of weapons and equipment to sustain this effort. The Cold War was largely fought in the imagination, at least in Europe, and so there were far fewer casualties, except in the proxy wars outside Europe.

The war in Vietnam (1965 to 1973) should have challenged the story.[1] In Vietnam, Americans faced what would now be called an asymmetric enemy. Insurgents fought a guerrilla war in which they avoided battle against a superior enemy. Instead they aimed to wear down the Americans and to win the "hearts and minds" of the population.

The heavy-handed American conception of war "as a crusade to be won quickly and completely . . . using high technology and almost unlimited firepower"[2] devastated the countryside and alienated the Vietnamese people, creating more recruits to the insurgency. The chilling metrics of the war were combat missions flown, numbers of targets achieved, and numbers of insurgents killed (many of them probably civilians). Technologies like herbicides to destroy food sources and napalm to burn villages remain seared on the history of that conflict.

The war caused a crisis in the American military establishment, with high levels of desertion, reported "fragging" (killing one's own officers), combat refusals, and drug addiction.[3] And growing awareness of what was going on, even before the Internet and satellite television, created a massive domestic opposition within the United States. In the end, the Americans were forced to withdraw and the insurgents, the Vietcong, backed by the government of North Vietnam, took over the country.

There were dissidents within the U.S. military at the time who proposed an alternative approach. In 1940, the U.S. Marines had published a manual entitled *Small Wars*, which proposed a different way of dealing with insurgencies, drawing on the colonial experience, especially the experience of the United States in the Philippines, and putting the emphasis on controlling local populations. But there was great resistance to changing course because the so-called "American Way of War" was so embedded in American military and industrial institutions. "I'll be damned if I permit the United States Army, its institutions and traditions, to be destroyed just to win this lousy war," said one senior officer.[4]

Of course, many articles and books written after Vietnam criticized the way the war was fought, arguing that less-destructive methods might have been more effective. But the defense establishment chose to learn a different lesson. They argued that the war was not destructive enough, and some even went so far as to suggest that nuclear weapons should have been used.

Colonel Harry Summers's 1982 book, *A Critical Analysis of the Vietnam War*, which made the case for an even more destructive approach, reflected the majority view within the military establishment.[5]

In the 1970s and 1980s, there were efforts to adapt American warfare to new technologies, particularly information and communications technologies. Terms like "AirLand Battle" and, later, the "Revolution in Military Affairs" were supposed to herald far-reaching technology-induced changes in the U.S. military. But actually, the technologies were integrated into existing doctrines and institutions. The new technologies were supposed to increase speed, accuracy, and destructiveness and, at the same time, to improve force protection. In particular, there was a growing emphasis on airpower as a way of demonstrating American military superiority without risking American casualties so that the kind of opposition that developed during the Vietnam years would not be repeated. This would become known in military circles as "Nintendo Warfare."

Learning the Wrong Lessons

The Cold War ended because the Soviet Union and Central Europe imploded. The central planning system was too rigid and could not assimilate new technology or increases in productivity. Communism had lost its ideological appeal. The Soviet army that intervened in Afghanistan in 1979 was forced to withdraw, with ruinous consequences for political and military morale. The Polish mass trades union, Solidarity, strongly supported by the Catholic Church, and the peace movement in East Germany that had developed under the umbrella of the Protestant churches had opened up new civil-society spaces and new demands in Eastern Europe.

The coming to power of Mikhail Gorbachev, who wanted to restructure the Soviet economy and society and to develop a new cooperative approach to foreign policy, set in motion an irreversible process that led to the collapse of communism.

Western leaders, political commentators, and foreign-policy scholars and specialists were stunned. For about a year, they agonized in think tanks, universities, and government departments about why they had failed to predict the end of the Cold War.

And then they came up with the answer—an answer seen through the prism of that glittering moment at the end of World War II: *America had "won" the Cold War!* Communism collapsed because the United States had stayed firm throughout the forty-year history of the Cold War, maintaining and upgrading a huge military capability that threatened the Soviet Union—in particular, a new generation of high-technology weapons, ordered by President Reagan, that the Soviet Union could not match. It was American resolve that had brought the Soviet Union to its knees.

"What is clear," proclaimed the *Wall Street Journal*, "is that in the fourth decade of the East's imprisonment, the U.S. and its allies determined to stand up more firmly than ever to the 'other force' and that the Soviet Union decided to stand down.'"[6] Or, as former national-security adviser Zbigniew Brzezinski put it: "The massive U.S. defense buildup of the early 1980s—including the decision to proceed with the Strategic Defense Initiative—both shocked the Soviets and then strained their resources."[7]

It was an argument that could not be refuted because there was no actual conflict. One could equally well argue that the Western threat had sustained communist power by helping to establish an us-versus-them mentality that strengthened the hardliners in the Kremlin. Indeed, it is more convincing to suggest that it was President Reagan's arms control offers—the zero option to get rid of medium range missiles and the strategic missile reductions—that provided an opportunity for change in the Soviet Union.

This kind of argument was to be repeated in every post–Cold War crisis. It explained why it was not necessary to dismantle the huge military-industrial edifice built up during World War II and the Cold War, and why the military did not need to change its philosophy about how to fight wars with overwhelming force.

Military spending did fall after the end of the Cold War, but spending on research and development—that is, on the military systems of the future—remained at the same level. In strategic think tanks and security consultancies, experts whose ideas had been formed by the Cold War were busy thinking up new enemies with new, inventive ways of attacking America—rogue states armed with missiles, lone terrorists armed with weapons of mass destruction—and new ways of capitalizing on America's "unipolar moment."

They did not actually anticipate 9/11, but it was the kind of scenario they had been imagining; indeed, the Project for the New American Century, which, along with the American Enterprise Institute and the Heritage Foundation, was to provide much of the intellectual input into George W. Bush's administration, suggested that the kind of defense build-up they envisaged would be difficult without some "catastrophic and catalyzing event like a new Pearl Harbor."[8]

The first post–Cold War crisis was the Gulf War of 1991, which provided a showy opportunity to exhibit the technological developments of the past two decades. In effect, it was a demonstration to the world of the Revolution in Military Affairs. After Saddam Hussein invaded Kuwait, the United States responded massively, with the support of the United Nations. Half a million Coalition troops were deployed in Saudi Arabia, and the Pentagon rolled out Operation 90-1002 (pronounced Ten-Oh-Two), which had been developed in the early 1980s to contain a southward thrust by the Soviet Union. Cruise missiles, laser-guided bombs, early GPS systems, and satellite imagery were all magnificently displayed. After years of war with Iran, Iraq had large numbers of poorly trained and poorly equipped soldiers, but not much else. In effect, Iraq was elevated to the status of superpower by the scale of forces arrayed against it.

This hugely expensive show resulted in the liberation of Kuwait with very few American casualties—some 148 American troops were killed, one-third of them by friendly fire. It seemed like a dazzling success for the combination of morality, massive firepower, and technological prowess. Very few people questioned whether Saddam Hussein could have been dealt with at less cost, in terms of money, deaths, and destruction, or in some other way. "One thing is clear," said President George H. W. Bush, "we have licked the Vietnam syndrome once and for all."[9]

American policy makers went on to draw similar conclusions about the importance of conventional military power, especially airpower, from the crisis in the former Yugoslavia. In the final stages of the Bosnian War, NATO airplanes bombed Serb positions. Even though by this time ethnic cleansing was largely complete and the map of Bosnia (and Croatia) had been largely reconfigured along ethnic lines, many U.S. policy makers regarded the bombing as decisive. In a speech he gave soon after the Dayton Peace Accords was signed, President Clinton argued that "[t]hose air strikes, together with the renewed determination of our European partners, and the Bosnian and Croat gains on the battlefield, convinced the Serbs, finally, to start thinking about making peace."[10] And according to the secretary of defense, William J. Perry, the air campaign "was an absolutely stunning development to them [the Serbs]. It totally demoralized them and drove them effectively to the peace table."[11]

That lesson drawn from the final stages of the Bosnian War was to be applied in Kosovo in 1999. Kosovo had been left out of the Dayton Peace Accords, which focussed on ending the War in Bosnia and Herzegovina, even though the crisis had been brewing since 1990, when Milosevic removed the autonomous status of Kosovo. Kosovar Albanians, who constituted 90 percent of the population, had been dismissed from public service and excluded from secondary schools and universities. The Albanian Kosovars, influenced by the peaceful 1989 revolutions, organized themselves in a nonviolent movement. They held their own referendum on independence in September 1991 and Kosovo-wide elections in May 1992. They organized a parallel education system as well as independent Albanian newspapers and NGOs for health care, human-rights monitoring, and other activities. And they funded all this through individual voluntary contributions from Kosovars both at home and abroad.

But by the late 1990s, the parallel system was becoming exhausted and a new group, the Kosovo Liberation Army (KLA), committed to violent strategies, began to gather adherents. As Veton

Surroi, one of the most significant independent intellectuals, put it, Dayton had demonstrated that "ethnic territories have legitimacy" and that "international attention can only be obtained through war."[12] An additional factor was the sudden availability of arms after the Albanian state collapsed in the summer of 1997; arms caches were opened and hundreds of thousands of Kalashnikovs were available for sale at a few dollars each. Many Kosovar Albanians abroad switched their donations to the "Homeland Calling" fund organized by the KLA.

Slobodan Milosevic responded with typical brutality, and there were widespread fears of large-scale ethnic cleansing on the Bosnian model. The extreme right-wing radical party that had been directly responsible for many of the atrocities in Bosnia and Herzegovina, led by Vojislav Seselj (who is now in The Hague awaiting trial), had joined the governing coalition in Serbia. Since 1991, the party had advocated the expulsion "without delay" of all Kosovar Albanians.

The method chosen by Western leaders to stop ethnic cleansing, as a result of their reading of the Bosnia conflict, was diplomacy— backed by the threat of air strikes. When diplomacy failed to stop the conflict, NATO responded with a 77-day air campaign. Altogether, some 36,000 sorties were flown, of which 12,000 were strike sorties. Some 20,000 "smart" bombs and 5,000 conventional bombs were dropped. But it appears that not much damage was done to the Yugoslav military machine. For fifty years, the Yugoslav army had been trained to withstand a superior enemy. A vast underground network had been built, including stores, airports, and barracks. Tactics had been developed that involved constructing decoys, hiding tanks and artillery, conserving air defenses, and avoiding troop concentrations. NATO did not succeed, in the initial stages, in knocking out the Yugoslav air-defense system; that is why NATO aircraft continued to fly at 15,000 feet.

NATO was more successful in hitting civilian targets—roads, bridges, power stations, oil depots, and factories. Because of the insistence that aircraft fly above 15,000 feet, pilots could not see what was happening on the ground and were dependent on intelligence from numerous, often badly coordinated, sources. Consequently, repeated mistakes were made, as became embarrassingly clear for the duration of the air strikes. Low points included the bombing of the Chinese Embassy and the bombing of refugees inside Kosovo. The killing of some 1,400 people was called "collateral damage." Environmental damage resulted from attacks on industrial facilities. Historic sites were destroyed in places such as Novi Sad. A TV transmitter was destroyed, and journalists in the building were killed. And targets were hit in Montenegro, whose government had refused to participate in the war in Kosovo.

Serbia used the bombing as a cover to accelerate ethnic cleansing. Many of the paramilitary groups that had undertaken the dirty work in Bosnia reappeared in Kosovo. During the bombing, 10,000 or so Albanians were killed; 863,000 civilians were forced to seek refuge outside Kosovo, and an additional 590,000 were internally displaced. Kosovar Albanians were subjected to widespread rape and torture as well as looting, pillaging, and extortion.[13] As General Wesley Clark, who commanded the NATO forces, put it: "air power alone cannot stop paramilitary murder on the ground and that's what's going on down there."[14]

In the end, Milosevic capitulated and agreed to NATO's demands. Right up until the last few days, no one expected that he would concede defeat. Crucial factors seem to have been the destruction of civilian infrastructure, the loss of support from some of Milosevic's inner circle, and, above all, the intervention of the Russians, who made it clear that they could not continue to support the Yugoslav position. It is also sometimes asserted that Milosevic was influenced by NATO discussions about ground intervention, although even if, as is claimed, a decision were imminent, it would have taken some time to organize.

The air strikes both contributed to the fall of Milosevic and, together with economic sanctions, helped to precipitate economic collapse, but they also helped to entrench embittered anti-Western nationalistic attitudes that persist to this day.

Western leaders were triumphant. "This is the first war for human rights," declared the British prime minister, Tony Blair.[15] "If one can say of any war that it is ethical, or that it is being waged for ethical reasons, then it is true of this war," said the Czech president and former dissident Vaclav Havel.[16] And according to Lloyd Axworthy, the Canadian foreign minister, "NATO prevailed over evil . . . The Alliance's intervention was an important step in the ascendance of human security as a norm for global action."[17] Indeed, the war seemed not only to reinforce the conservative view that technologically advanced conventional military force is the way to defeat America's enemies, but it also attracted liberals to the idea that conventional military force could be used for humanitarian purposes.

The lessons that were drawn from the Gulf War, Bosnia, and Kosovo reproduced the twentieth-century mindset—the idea that conventional military force can be used to prevail over enemies and to promote democracy and human rights. The lessons of the intervention in Somalia in 1992, which ended in debacle, were ignored. U.S. forces went to Somalia in the midst of a "new war" to deliver humanitarian aid and provide food security. However, attacks on Pakistani troops led the American commander, Admiral Jonathan Howe, to engage in warfare against the clan faction responsible, led by General Aideed. Despite the use of what many considered to be excessive force, the Americans failed to capture Aideed.

On the contrary, Somali militia succeeded in shooting down two American helicopters, killing eighteen American soldiers and wounding seventy-five. The bodies of the American soldiers were paraded publicly in front of international television cameras. Shortly thereafter, the Clinton administration decided to withdraw from Somalia. The failure of the Somali intervention was one reason the Clinton administration was so reluctant to intervene in the Rwandan genocide.

That Americans chose to learn some lessons and not others has to be explained in terms of the deeply embedded structures of the American way of war. This is not a conspiratorial argument about vested interests. Rather it is about how narratives of power are built into the ways institutions function. The wrong lessons are rewarded in institutional and career terms. People who work in institutions—the armed forces, the defense industry, bureaucracies, Congress, the media—tend to reinforce each others' received wisdom and by so doing reproduce their careers. American leaders made successive misjudgments about the value of force because their thinking was so bound up in the unique success of World War II and their experiences were shaped by the institutions established during that period and sustained by the Cold War.

Beebe experienced this deep-rooted thinking first hand. When, in the mid-1990s, he returned from an assignment in Germany, where he had watched Somalia, the beginnings of the Balkan conflict, and Haiti unravel, he attended the U.S. Army Field Artillery Advanced Course. One day, he and several hundred other captains gathered in Snow Hall to hear a senior Army general discuss his vision of the future and what young officers should be prepared for. He spoke of the importance of being physically fit and ready to lead soldiers into combat. He spoke of the downsizing of the Army.

He also spoke of the future of the field artillery with the new Crusader Howitzer. This system would be able to attack and kill more with less personnel. It would also be the heaviest self-propelled 155mm howitzer ever built—almost twice the weight of its predecessor. This would be necessary to keep ahead of "near-peer" threats of the twenty-first century, claimed the general.

During the question-and-answer session, Beebe posed a simple question: "Do you think conflict of the twenty-first century will be like what we've seen in Somalia, Haiti, or the Balkans, where this weapon system will have little relevance in an urban environment?"

The general chuckled a little, as did some of the other captains. The general looked at Beebe and replied, "Son, don't take your eye off the ball with all this other silliness going on right now. The Army is not the world's policeman. You stay focused on what you're trained to do, and that's kill the enemy that's preparing right now to do the same to you." Beebe sat down, a bit ashamed that he'd asked such a question.

There was, during this period, other thinking within the United Nations, within the European Union, in Canada and Japan—much of it along the lines of human security. Even in Russia, at that time, there was much interest in the idea of common security. In Eastern Europe, the human-rights ideals of those who had led the 1989 revolutions had much resonance even though governments (often former communists tagged by Rumsfeld as "new Europe") passionately supported the American idea of security. But the United States was the dominant power, and U.S. administrations were setting the global agenda. The last unfettered expression of twentieth century thinking and language, misapplied to a twenty-first-century problem, came after September 11, 2001. President George W. Bush declared that in response to the attacks, his administration would fight a "War on Terror"—and, he might as well have added, fight it the old-fashioned way, because that is what happened.

4

The Wars in Afghanistan and Iraq

Given the persistence of the twentieth-century mindset, it is perhaps not surprising that President George W. Bush reacted to 9/11 the way he did. In speech after speech he compared the events of September 11, 2001, to the Japanese attack on Pearl Harbor in December 1941 and called on Americans to reenact the courage of earlier generations.

"On September the 11th, 2001," he said in one typical speech, "our nation woke up to another sudden attack plotted in secret and executed without mercy. In the space of just 102 minutes, more Americans were killed than we lost at Pearl Harbor. Like generations before us, we accepted new responsibilities, and we confronted new dangers with firm resolve ... [W]e will fight this war without wavering, and like the generations before us, we will prevail ... Like earlier struggles for freedom, this war will take many turns. And the enemy must be defeated on every battle front, from the streets of Western cities to the mountains of Afghanistan, to the tribal regions of Pakistan, to the islands of Southeast Asia and the Horn of Africa."[1]

The application of conventional military force in situations that were characterized by twenty-first century conditions made those conditions much worse. In effect, it was the card pulled out of the fragile house of cards, the tipping point for a "new war" in both Afghanistan and Iraq.

The invasions of Afghanistan (2001) and Iraq (2003) appeared, momentarily, to be huge successes for the twentieth-century mantra. They seemed to confirm the lessons that policymakers chose to learn from Kosovo: that military force can be used to liberate people as well as to defeat enemies.

The invasion of Afghanistan, which quickly followed the events of 9/11, had widespread international sympathy. It involved the use of U.S. airpower allied to the Northern Alliance, and local forces who opposed the Taliban. American forces did not succeed in capturing Osama bin Laden, but they destroyed the terrorist camps where Al-Qaeda operatives had been trained, and they toppled the vicious, misogynist Taliban regime. In the case of Iraq, by contrast, there was widespread global opposition and the attempt to garner United Nations approval failed. Nevertheless, U.S. and British forces invaded Iraq over a short three-week period and succeeded in overthrowing the regime of Saddam Hussein. President Bush claimed that the invasion of Iraq marked "the arrival of a new era,"[2] in which, thanks to information technology, war had become rapid, precise, and low in casualties. Max Boot, writing in *Foreign Affairs*, described the invasion as "dazzling": "That the United States and its allies won anyway—and won so quickly—must rank as one of the single achievements of military history."[3] Donald Rumsfeld, the secretary of defense, talked about "overmatching" power as opposed to "overwhelming" power:

> In the twenty-first century, mass may no longer be the best measure of power in a conflict. After all, when Baghdad fell, there were

just over 100,000 American forces on the ground. General Franks overwhelmed the enemy not with the typical three-to-one advantage in mass but by overmatching the enemy with advanced capabilities in innovative and unexpected ways.[4]

Actually, Western forces had entered both countries, by and large, with the consent of the local populations. In Iraq, there was almost no resistance. The Iraqi army and the Republican Guard melted away. The Americans dropped leaflets in Arabic telling soldiers to take off their uniforms and go home, and most of them obeyed. There was, as one commentator put it, an "unpleasant, short-lived episode of violent irregular combat" in the third week of March, when *Firqat Fedayeen Saddam* (Saddam's Martyrs) and other small units established to defend the regime tried to resist, but not much more.[5]

The situation appeared calm initially not because the Coalition Forces controlled the country but because the Iraqi people were ready to give the Coalition Forces the benefit of the doubt. In other words, the invasion was more like an exercise than a war. Precisely because the invasions were so easy, the Americans, in both Afghanistan and Iraq, only controlled their own bases.

Toppling regimes is not the same as building democracy. Afghanistan and Iraq are very different countries. Afghanistan is one and a half times the size of Iraq and largely rural. It is one of the poorest countries in the world. The life expectancy of an average Afghan is forty-three years; less than a third of the population, and only 12 percent of women, can read and write.

By contrast, Iraq is largely urban, with a sophisticated, highly educated middle class and, before the wars and sanctions, a world-class health system. Indeed, Iraq is one of the oldest civilizations in the world; arithmetic was invented there and the House of Wisdom, which Kaldor visited in 2004, is the oldest think tank in the world, founded in the ninth century.

But what Afghanistan and Iraq had in common at the time of the invasions was that they were both on the verge of state collapse. Afghanistan had always had a weak state dependent on revenue from outside powers, and the national government exercised limited control outside Kabul. Decades of war, involving physical destruction and large-scale population displacement, had greatly weakened both traditional governance structures and the capacity of the state.

In the case of Iraq, both President Bush, advised by the exiled opposition, and Saddam Hussein had a common interest in portraying the Iraqi regime as a classic totalitarian system, controlling every aspect of society and only removable by force.[6]

But in fact, at the time of the invasion, the regime exhibited characteristics that are typical of the last phases of totalitarianism—a system that is breaking up under the impact of globalization, unable to sustain its closed, autarchic, tightly controlled character. After two major wars and the imposition of economic sanctions, tax revenue had declined dramatically, as had the provision of services. The last years of Saddam's rule saw the rise of tribalism, as he made deals with tribal leaders to maintain power; the spread of criminality because of both sanctions and the failures of the command economy; and the emergence of sectarian politics, both ethnic and religious, as Ba'athist ideology lost its appeal.

The invasions of both countries effectively destroyed not just the regimes but what was left of the states as well. In Afghanistan, the security forces were undermined by infiltration of the militias that had assisted the Americans in toppling the regime. In addition, the small civil service fell apart as the huge international effort diverted skills and knowledge so that poorly paid government employees were ready to take lower-level but better-paid positions (e.g., as drivers or interpreters) in international agencies or NGOs.[7] In Iraq, the newly established Coalition Provisional Authority further undermined the state by two decrees. First they dismissed all former members of the Ba'ath Party, effectively denuding government service of all skilled people, since membership in the Ba'ath Party had been a necessary condition for promotion. Secondly they dismantled the army, thereby removing the one unifying security service and humiliating and impoverishing the very people who had taken off their uniforms and allowed the Americans to intervene (and who still had access to weapons).

Conventional military force cannot rebuild states. At the time of the invasions, the general view in the United States, expressed forcefully by both Colin Powell, the secretary of state, and his successor, Condoleezza Rice, was that the job of the military was fighting wars and that soldiers should not be used for what Powell dismissively called "constabulary duties."[8] "The President must remember," wrote Rice in *Foreign Affairs*, "that the military is a special instrument. It is lethal and it is meant to be. It is not a civilian peace force. It is not a political referee. And it is most certainly not designed to build a civilian society."[9] The result of this kind of thinking was a security vacuum and the beginnings of the vortex of violence. While the Americans in Afghanistan continued to hunt for Al-Qaeda leaders through Operation Enduring Freedom, the internationally authorizd NATO force, ISAF (International Security Assistance Force), which might have acted as a "peace force," was initially confined to Kabul. In Iraq, the Americans did nothing to prevent the widespread looting that followed the invasion (except to protect the oil ministry and oil installations), allowing the loss of irreplaceable ancient objects and manuscripts from museums that are part of the world's civilizational heritage. "Stuff happens," was Donald Rumsfeld's famously laconic response.

Nor was there a serious civilian effort to reconstruct the state. Much more was done in Afghanistan than in Iraq. The United Nations led a nation-building process based on the Bonn Agreement, which had brought together all of the different Afghan factions and power brokers except the Taliban. Even so, the process was hampered by the continued American reliance on the Northern Alliance, which brought the former commanders (or warlords) and their militias into the government, and also by the lack of security outside Kabul.

In Iraq, inexperienced Republican staffers sat in the protected green zone—a large area of Baghdad where the Coalition Provisional Authority was based. Grass and palm trees, fountains and pools, palaces and rose gardens offered a calm environment for coalition staff, who were beavering away, trying to introduce "off the shelf" models of democracy in Iraq. They developed a twelve-step plan for introducing democracy, and one official told Kaldor in November 2003 that "we have to finish this quickly because we know best how to do democracy; political pressure will force us to hand over sovereignty to Iraqis who don't know how to do it as well as us." At that time there were signs all over the green zone saying "What have you done for Iraq today?" Kaldor met consultants running training courses on how to be a civil servant with flip charts and "facilitated session techniques." As the instructors explained what they were doing, they kept stumbling over the name of the country, confusing it with the various places where they had done the same thing—Croatia, Bosnia, Sierra Leone, Angola, Afghanistan.... And millions of dollars were being spent on American contractors like Creative Associates International, Inc., and Research Triangle International, who were supposed to teach Iraqis how to have civil society.

Traveling around the red zone (i.e., unsafe areas in Iraq) in 2003 and 2004, Kaldor met with many groups, including the intellectuals in the House of Wisdom, women's groups who had organized support for the victims of Saddam Hussein, and student groups who were building their own dormitories after American

forces had commandeered the university dormitories. She visited
the Hewar (Dialogue) Art Gallery, which was established by a well-
known artist who left the Ba'ath Party at the time of the invasion
of Kuwait. Here, artists could exhibit their work and meet and talk
with foreign buyers in a café. Kaldor drank dried-lime tea with
artists from the group Najeen (Survivors), who had openly opposed
the regime. She also talked to the Council of Muslim Clerics—
the Sunni clerics who were the main source of political and moral
authority for many of those who had been implicated in the
Ba'athist regime and who were to become the backbone of the insurgency. The meeting took place in a huge mosque that had been
built in celebration of the "mother of all battles" (Saddam Hussein's description of the first Gulf war). The cavernous structure
featured minarets designed to look like rockets and was built
around water in the shape of the Arab world.

But few of these people had much contact with the Coalition
Forces and their partners, hidden away in the green zone. Instead,
the Coalition Forces relied on expats like the former halal butcher
from North London whom Kaldor met who was made policy plan-
ner in the newly created ministry of defense. When an interim Iraqi
government was eventually established, along with a political
process leading to elections, it was organized largely by a bevy of
foreign and Iraqi-exile advisers who rarely left the green zone. Moreover, influenced by the experience of the former Yugoslavia, the
political process was heavily shaped by ethno-sectarian considera-
tions so that when, in 2005, elections did take place, electoral
choices were defined in sectarian terms—there were separate Kurdish, Shi'ia, and Sunni lists.

In other words, the invasions created a security and political vacuum into which rushed the typical actors of a "new war," the elements of a twenty-first-century vortex of violence, or what has been
called a "complex adaptive system"—"sprawling multi-organiza-

tional networks" that have the capacity to communicate with each other and adapt.[10] One element of the vortex of violence is, of course, the insurgencies, whose stated goal is to end the occupation of both countries. In Iraq, the bulk of the insurgency was Iraqi nationalist and Sunni Islamist and arose more or less spontaneously starting in the summer of 2003. The most important recruits were former military personnel. Their weapon of choice was the roadside bomb, or the improvised explosive device (IED), which became increasingly sophisticated over the course of the insurgency.

In Afghanistan, the majority of the insurgents are members of the Taliban based in the southern part of the country. There are also smaller insurgent groups in other areas—for instance, the Haqqani network (linked to a series of daring attacks like the Serena Hotel bombing in January 2008 and the attempted assassination of President Karzai) and Gulbuddin Hekmatyar's Hezb-i-Islami, which has been fighting since the Soviet occupation. As in Iraq, these groups fuse nationalism with a severe form of Salafist Islam, which harks back to the early years of Islam.

Al-Qaeda is present in both Iraq and Afghanistan, although it was not evident in Iraq before the March 2003 invasion.[11] Al-Qaeda is a global organization and is much more antipolitical than the locally based insurgent groups. In effect, its goal is the struggle against the West. It specializes in grisly, well-publicized attacks, especially suicide attacks, and in communications and information. The invasions of both Afghanistan and Iraq acted as a magnet for jihadists all over the world and have greatly expanded their field of operations and opportunities for training and experience.

It was Al-Qaeda that was responsible for gruesome public executions of Western hostages, and it was Al-Qaeda that fomented the sectarian violence in Iraq, so that the insurgency morphed into a civil war, with spectacular attacks on Shi'ia areas and monuments. The most celebrated was the bombing of the Golden Dome

Mosque in Samarra, one of the most important Shi'ia shrines in the world, on February 26, 2006.

Another element of the vortex of violence is local militias of various kinds. There are tribal militias in Afghanistan and Iraq. Tribes are often considered traditional structures, but in both countries tribes have been reinvented in response to colonialism, war, and the modern state. Thus, in Iraq, tribes are really common-interest groups with some element of clan or kinship. Whereas traditional tribes were rural organizations, in Iraq, rural-urban tribal networks developed during the Saddam period both, because Saddam Hussein increasingly relied on the tribes for security, and because personal ties became more important with the decline of social welfare and the crushing of civil society.[12] Many tribal militias were linked to insurgent groups. For example, the Zobai tribe was closely associated with the Revolutionary Brigades and the Islamic Army of Iraq. In Afghanistan, tribes have sustained local networks and often work with the Taliban and other insurgent groups, partly out of fear and partly because they are disillusioned with the Afghan government.

In Afghanistan, there are also militias controlled by former commanders who are now allied to the government or even part of the government, serving as provincial governors or ministers. Consider the case of Abdul Rashid Dostum, the Uzbek warlord who controlled a northern fiefdom before 2001 and who led the horsemen who liberated Mazar-i-Sharif in 2001 with great brutality. (Hundreds of his captives were locked inside containers and suffocated to death.) Until 2008, he was commander in chief of the Afghan army. Other commanders include Nazir Mohammed, who runs the provincial capital Faizabad and whose militias are supposed to protect NATO, and Ismail Khan, who dominates the western city of Herat.

In Iraq, probably the most important armed militias are attached to political parties and are part of the sectarian competition to control the state apparatus. The Peshmerger are attached to the Kurdish parties who resisted Saddam Hussein in the north. Some militias were created by parties in exile; the most important of these is the Badr Corps, which is attached to the Islamic Supreme Council of Iraq (ISCI) and trained by the Iranian Revolutionary Guard. Of the militias created since 2001, the most important is the Mahdi army of Muqtada al-Sadr, known as Jaish al-Mahdi (JAM). Both the Badr Corps and the JAM infiltrated the ministry of interior and the police between 2005 and 2007. One of the former commanders of the Badr Corps, Bayan Jabr, was minister of the interior from 2005 to 2006.

Starting in 2005, these Iraqi groups engaged in sectarian violence and ethnic cleansing reminiscent of the Yugoslav wars. While the Sunni groups favored the use of explosives in Shi'ia areas or monuments, the Shi'ia groups used death squads to kill prominent Sunnis in spectacular ways and to take over neighborhoods, expelling the residents. They would seize Sunni properties, including houses, villas, and stores that had belonged to the Baghdad bourgeoisie since Ottoman times, and rent them to Shi'ia families or loot them. They would extort money from local merchants, festoon the area with Shi'ia flags, and infiltrate, co-opt, or replace the local police. They would take over gas stations and control the essential sale of gas, propane, and kerosene. And they would levy extensive local "taxation," in effect setting up a sort of parallel system. Intellectuals and people in the middle class were particularly targeted; hundreds of academics were killed during the worst of the violence.

A third element of the vortex of violence is criminal groups. In Iraq, Saddam Hussein released criminals from prison shortly before the invasion. The most important criminal activity is oil smuggling, which can take various forms, including siphoning off oil at its source and drilling holes in pipelines. During the height of the violence, tribes who were paid to protect pipelines developed a profitable business, siphoning the oil before protecting the pipeline. Other groups were involved in smuggling historic artifacts, taking hostages, kidnapping for ransom, looting, and pillaging. In Afghanistan, the most important criminal activity is the production and sale of opium. Afghanistan is responsible for some 93 percent of the world's poppy production, largely concentrated in the south and linked to the Taliban. Criminal groups are also engaged in timber smuggling, illicit gem smuggling, human trafficking, kidnapping, and taking hostages.

All of these groups are interrelated. The insurgents and the militias are involved in crime to finance their organizations. And the criminal groups use political violence as a cover for their criminal activities. The insurgents are engaged in internal political violence, and many of the militias, especially JAM, are also part of the insurgency. Many of these groups are organized into loosely connected networks of cells with more or less centralized discipline. None of them are confined to Iraq and Afghanistan. Al-Qaeda is, of course, a global network, recruiting young men throughout the Middle East and Europe as well as Asia. The Afghan groups mostly operate from Pakistan and have close ties with both Pakistani groups and the Pakistan intelligence service Inter-Services Intelligence (ISI), which helped to build up the mujahideen during the Soviet occupation and supported the Taliban. The Iraqi groups, both insurgents and militias, receive money and technical expertise from Iran, Saudi Arabia, and Syria. Iran seems to have helped to develop increasingly sophisticated IEDs for all sides. All of the groups also depend on remittances from families abroad.

Thus the violence in Iraq and Afghanistan involves a multifaceted, shifting pattern of attacks against American forces and their allies, widespread human-rights violations by warlords and their militias, and, of course, criminal violence—the deadly components of a twenty-first-century vortex of violence, or a "new war." While some participants may have specific political goals, others are using the nexus of violence and criminality to enrich themselves, and yet others are using it as an opportunity to settle personal scores or merely for excitement. It is sometimes assumed that the cycle of violence involves an ever-deepening cycle of retaliation as one group seeks revenge for an attack by the other and vice versa. But actually the attacks can be viewed as a sort of legitimization for violence that is usually directed at civilians rather than against other fighting groups. In other words, the cycle of violence provides a sort of cover, a sanction for illicit and brutal behaviour.

The fundamental problem has been the inability to establish effective institutions of law and order. In Iraq, the government is composed of a coalition of sectarian interests who cannot agree on shared policy, and who infiltrate the security sector, even though since mid-2007 some steps have been taken to establish a more centralized nationalist government. In Afghanistan, the problem of impunity for commanders, not just for past crimes, but for what is happening now, erodes any legitimacy President Karzai might have once enjoyed. Because there is no trust in government (or in outside forces), people turn to local strongmen, insurgents, and militias for protection.

The main victims of all this violence are civilians. The killing of civilians in American attacks is considered "collateral damage." Civilians are killed in insurgent attacks because they do not have the same protection as soldiers. They are the victims of human-rights violations and ethnic cleansing. One of the most telling aspects of this sorry story that illustrates the value that is put on the lives of American and British soldiers is that no one knows the full extent of civilian casualties.

The deaths of soldiers are carefully recorded, but civilian deaths are not counted. Iraq Body Count, which is based on media reports, estimated that over 90,000 civilians had been killed in Iraq up to April 2009. Figures estimated by the British medical journal *The Lancet*, using the epidemiological method of interviewing sample families, are much higher. They suggest some 650,000 excess deaths between March 2003 and the middle of 2006, of which over 600,000 were due to violence.[13] The really intense period of violence when 3,000 to 4,000 people were killed each month from mid-2005 to mid-2007 was after the period of the *Lancet* estimate.

In Afghanistan, systematic collection of civilian fatality data only began in 2007. The United Nations now maintains a database, but it is not publicly accessible. According to the UN Assistance Mission in Afghanistan (UNAMA), some 1,523 people were killed in 2007 and 2,118 in 2008 (these numbers are thought to be an underestimate by Afghan NGOs particularly the Independent Commission on Human Rights). According to these figures, slightly more people were killed by the Taliban and their allies than by NATO and government forces. Thirty-two percent of casualties were the result of suicide and IED attacks; 24 percent were the result of air strikes; and 20 percent were criminal murders.[14]

In Iraq, some 4 million people were forced to leave their homes; half went abroad.

Afghans constitute the largest refugee population in the world, mostly as a result of earlier wars and the Taliban regime. Since 2001, over 4 million refugees returned to Afghanistan. Yet, as of January 2007, the Congressional Research Service estimates that there are probably 3.5 million registered and unregistered Afghans still in Pakistan and Iran, 2.46 million in the former and nearly 1 million in the latter.[15] And many returned refugees are leaving again. Official estimates suggest that there are also over 200,000 internally displaced persons (IDPs), of which over half were displaced by earlier tragedies. However, the number of IDPs seems to have increased sharply from 2007 especially in the south of the country.[16]

The conventional military tactics adopted by American military forces were a significant contributing factor to the violence. Both during and after the invasions, the United States adopted "old war" tactics in complex, twenty-first-century, "new war" conditions. In pursuing Al-Qaeda and the Taliban in Afghanistan and in responding to the growing insurgency in Iraq, American military forces largely stayed in their bases, venturing out primarily to attack the enemy. Confronted with the brutal reality of the insurgencies, coalition troops seemed to default to military logic. As in earlier, similar counterinsurgency efforts in Vietnam and Algeria: the excessive use of force; widespread detention, torture, and abuse as a means of extracting information; and hatred on both sides inevitably followed. The pictures of torture at Abu Ghraib were published while Kaldor was in Iraq, but they made much less impact there since reports of torture and abuse were already widespread.

The events in Fallujah in April 2004 illustrate the overriding nature of military logic in the early years of the war in Iraq. The Marines Expeditionary Force had recently replaced the 82nd Airborne as the force in charge of this restive city. The Marines went to Fallujah with the explicit intention of turning a new page, trying to win over the population while isolating the insurgents who used the city as a base from which to launch attacks throughout the country. The Marine commander confidently predicted that his troops would be playing football with the locals in a few weeks. What happened, however, was the exact opposite. An attempt to surgically remove the terrorists gradually deteriorated into a siege and an all-out war when four American security contractors were killed and their bodies mutilated in front of television cameras.

The use of punitive measures, heavy weapons, and indiscriminate fire quickly united the people of Fallujah behind the insurgents and indeed most of Iraq behind Fallujah. The use of white phosphorus horrified observers and raised the specter of Vietnam all over again.

Iraqis were pushed to rally behind their worst enemies—assorted Arab jihadists and regime loyalists who gathered there from all over the country. Once they started taking casualties, the Marines' overriding objective turned from winning hearts and minds to avenging fallen comrades, "pacify[ing] the city," and "finish[ing] the job." Only intense political pressure allowed the establishment of the cease-fire that paved the way for the subsequent security arrangement whereby control of the city was handed over to a former Republican Guard commander. The anti-American sentiment caused by the attack allowed insurgents including Abu Musab al-Zarqawi, the leader of Al-Qaeda in Iraq, to return to the city. And in November 2004, U.S. forces attacked again, causing the displacement of hundreds of thousands of people, much physical destruction, and thousands of civilian casualties.

Fallujah confirmed, for many Iraqis, an overriding impression that soon everyone's house would be broken into, civilians fired upon, and young men arbitrarily arrested. It was not possible to be in Iraq in the early years after the invasion without experiencing firsthand the nervy young soldiers at checkpoints and searches. Kaldor's car was stopped and searched because of a tip-off saying that someone in a black Opel was about to blow up the Sheraton Hotel. At every checkpoint, ominous signs warned in English and Arabic that troops were "Authorized to use live fire." In addition, of course, people were afraid of the presence of the Coalition Forces because they are targets for terrorist attacks and because of their habit of shooting indiscriminately when attacked.

It was this experience of Coalition Forces' casual attitude toward civilian casualties; the practice of detaining young men, undermining their dignity and inadvertently creating opportunities for them to be recruited to the various armed groups; and lack of respect for civilians — combined with a general absence of jobs and normal activities — that contributed to burgeoning insurgencies in Iraq and Afghanistan under cover of which other kinds of sectarian and criminal violence started to evolve. In Iraq, the perception that the Americans were on the side of the Shi'ia helped to foment sectarian conflict. Above all, the conventional military approach makes it extremely difficult to gather useful intelligence that might guide a more effective approach. Sitting in their compounds or in the green zone, American commanders simply did not know what was going on; they only had satellite information, which helped them pinpoint the whereabouts of specific enemies, but did nothing to increase their understanding of the politics.

"There were 130,000 U.S. troops in Iraq [in 2006]," wrote Thomas Ricks, "but they were becoming irrelevant as fighting swirled around the tall walls of their bases. To a surprising degree, they were off-stage and ill-informed. U.S. military intelligence gathering tended to focus on two sorts of events, anything that affected American troops and the killing of Iraqis. Other action affecting Iraqi civilians — kidnappings, rape, robberies, acts of extortion, and other forms of intimidation — didn't appear on the U.S. radar. As one soldier in the 4th infantry brigade put it, all that was 'background noise.'"[17]

According to Ricks, the "old war" in Iraq ended on November 19, 2005, when a Marine squad went on a killing spree after being hit by a roadside bomb in Haditha; they killed twenty-four Iraqis, including children. The subsequent report by Army Major General Eldon A. Bargewell found that the killings had been carried out "indiscriminately" and that the leaders of the Marine command thought it was the right approach: "All levels of command tended to view civilian casualties, even if in significant numbers, as routine."[18] This was the event that started a rethinking of the military approach that was to be associated with the surge in Iraq, although not yet in Afghanistan.

Learning the Right Lessons?

On January 10, 2007, President Bush announced a new military plan for Iraq, known as the surge. The surge in Iraq was not just about an increase in the number of troops, it was a profound change in strategy and tactics, based on, to use the jargon, a "population-centric approach." It sounded akin to human security, but in certain important respects it wasn't. The change in strategy was associated with General David H. Petraeus, who took over the command of the multinational forces in Iraq later that same month. It emphasized the protection of civilians over and above the protection of military forces, and bottom-up local security over and above technology and firepower.

The ideas and proposals for a change of strategy did not only come from General Petraeus. They had bubbled up from middle-level officers with experience on the ground, intellectuals who study defense, and people involved in civilian affairs. Web sites like the *Small Wars Journal* and blogs by soldiers in the field testified to the change of heart. The ideas did not only come from people who were frustrated with what was happening in Iraq and Afghanistan. Some of the ideas were informed by experiences in Central America—Panama, Haiti, and Colombia—and the Balkans.

Petraeus corralled many ideas and tried to bring about a change in organizational culture so that they could be put into practice. Before taking over the Iraqi command, Petraeus had been commander of the Combined Arms Center at Fort Leavenworth, Kansas. He used his time there to produce a new counterinsurgency manual. He took personal charge of the manual and emphasized the process of creating it, which brought together academics, human-rights activists, and military and civilian practitioners, as much as the final product. The manual, which was published in December 2006, turned out to be a powerful critique of the tactics used in Iraq, using some language associated with a human security approach.[19] It emphasized the key objective of legitimacy and establishing a government that can guarantee a rule of law. It put protection of civilians at the heart of the doctrine. It argued for an "appropriate level of force," suggesting, "Sometimes the more force you use the less effective it is"; "[s]ome of the best weapons for Counter-insurgency do not shoot"; and "[s]ometimes the more you protect your force the less secure you will be."[20] It also called for the integration of military and civilian activities.

When Kaldor interviewed General Petraeus in March 2009, he argued that counterinsurgency is the same as human security. The two key principles, he said, are

- Secure and serve the population
- Separate the reconcilables from the irreconcilables

The engine of change is the development of ideas. Although he serves in the Army, Petraeus has always been connected to the "small wars" current in the U.S. Marines. By writing the new counterinsurgency manual, he was able to change the curriculum at Fort Leavenworth.

Elements of the new strategy in Iraq had already been tried out in Tal Afar by Colonel H. R. McMaster and in Ramadi by Colonel Sean MacFarland. While the focus was on Baghdad, the strategy involved the establishment in many Iraqi cities of joint security stations staffed by U.S. and Iraqi soldiers and Iraqi police. In Sunni areas, the aim was to make it harder for Shi'ia militias to infiltrate. And in Shi'ia areas, "gated communities" were established with perimeter security measures such as barriers, walls, and checkpoints and with hardened markets, shops, and public places to prevent explosive attacks by Sunnis. The joint security stations were also supposed to provide a way of mentoring Iraqi forces and ensuring that they performed better; at the same time, the presence of Iraqis may have helped to improve American attitudes toward Iraqi civilians. Petraeus's injunction to "live amongst the people" was of key importance. And this was not just a matter of improved knowledge and understanding of the situation, it also led to greater empathy and respect for Iraqis. As one senior officer told Kaldor, "Everyone has a humanitarian conscience in the end."

A key feature of the new strategy was the treatment of detainees. "You had to identify the hard core and remove them," General Petraeus told Kaldor, "and it resulted in a transformation in behavior. We introduced a new program in the camps including moderation in religion, civic education, literacy, and sports. Some 18,000 were released last year [2008]. There are now less than 14,000 in Camp Bucca. Only 200 had to be rearrested; that's much lower than in U.S. prisons."

Despite these efforts, violence continued to intensify until the middle of 2007. Two factors were responsible for the drop in violence after July 2007. One was the *Awakening*. This was the change of sides by the Sunni tribes. The Sunni tribes had begun to distance themselves from Al-Qaeda as early as 2005. There were plenty of reasons. They rejected some of Al-Qaeda's more horrific tactics and didn't like Al-Qaeda's version of Islam. They objected to the way Al-Qaeda was muscling in on their communities and, in particular, taking control of their sources of revenue. One story has it that Al-Qaeda killed a sheikh who refused to give daughters of his tribe to them in marriage. Some tribes first approached the U.S. Marines for help in defeating Al-Qaeda in 2005, but it was not until the end of 2006 that the U.S. forces responded to these overtures. Before that, tribal efforts had failed disastrously and led to great brutality and intimidation from Al-Qaeda. The first concerted campaign was in Ramadi, and it had a dramatic effect on security. Sheikh Sattar al-Rishawi, a smuggler and highway robber of the Dulaimi tribe, joined with Fasal al-Gaoud, a former governor of Anbar whose Hamza forces came from the Albu Mahal tribe, to establish the Anbar Salvation Council. After joining forces with the Americans, Sattar was made "counterinsurgency coordinator" and the tribal militias were named "emergency response units." (Despite, or maybe because of his efforts, Sattar was assassinated in September 2007.) Newly created neighborhood-watch organizations — euphemistically called "concerned local citizens" or, as the militias preferred, "sons of Iraq" — began providing information, protecting families, and patrolling streets along with the Shi'ia-dominated army and police. They were paid $360 a month by the Americans. The model was copied throughout Iraq.

The other factor was the Sadrist cease-fire of August 2007. The reasons for the cease-fire are various: ethnic cleansing in Baghdad was virtually complete; the decline in Sunni violence had weakened Sadrist legitimacy; the Sadrist militias were becoming more undisciplined, acting more and more autonomously, and needed to be reined in; and there was a growing popular backlash against Sadrist tactics. Muqtada's orders for a cease-fire were largely obeyed; this led to a dramatic fall in anti-Sunni violence.

What was the role of the new U.S. strategy in all this? In the end, Iraqis themselves were substantially responsible for the decline in violence. But the presence of Coalition Forces on the streets (which drew Al-Qaeda fire away from Shi'ia communities) helped to lift the pall of fear; the provision of basic services; American responsiveness to Sunni overtures; the readiness of Coalition Forces to act as local mediators—all of these things may have created space in which deals could be made. The decline in violence was the result of local cease-fires made with some 779 militias composed of 10 to 800 men each. As David Kilcullen, General Petraeus's counterinsurgency adviser, put it,

> The original concept of the Joint Campaign Plan was that we [the Coalition and the Iraqi government] would create security, which would in turn create space for a "grand bargain" at the national level. Instead, in 2007, we saw the exact opposite: a series of local political deals displaced extremists, resulting in a major improvement in security at the local level, and the national government then began to jump on board with the program. Instead of Coalition-led top-down reconciliation, this process is Iraqi-led, bottom-up and based on civil society rather than national politics.[21]

General Petraeus has insisted that the decline in violence is fragile. Much depends on whether the government can overcome its sectarian character and act on behalf of Iraqis as a whole, on whether the Sunni constituency feels represented, on whether enough tribal militias can be integrated into the security services, on whether the demands of the poor who are attracted to the Sadrist movement can be met, and on whether the issue of the status of Northern Iraq, especially the role of Kirkuk, can be resolved. Many have warned of the dangers of embracing the "concerned local citizens," or "sons of Iraq," groups and of ceding control of some areas to informal tribal structures. "You have taken a crocodile as a pet," one Iraqi official warned. Prime Minister Nouri al-Maliki has managed to establish himself as a national leader, not least because of the action he took against Shi'ia militias in Basra (described in the next chapter). But in 2009, there was a sinister spike in Sunni violence against Shi'ia areas—probably a prelude to elections by tribal, sectarian, and criminal elements who hope to unseat the present government.

Petraeus was subsequently appointed as commander of the U.S. Central Command, which oversees both Iraq and Afghanistan. Can the strategy used in Iraq be applied in Afghanistan? Petraeus is the first to point out that no two situations are the same, even though the principles of counterinsurgency as he interprets it (secure and serve the population; separate the reconcilables from the irreconcilables) remain relevant. There is much hope that tribal militias who fight alongside the Taliban out of fear, as a source of income, or because they do not trust the Afghan government can be weaned away from the Taliban at local levels. One of General Petraeus's first acts was to issue a tactical directive reducing the use of air strikes.

General Stanley McChrystal, the commander in Afghanistan since June 2009, produced a comprehensive report in August 2009 proposing an integrated military-civilian campaign. The plan goes even further than Petraeus's counterinsurgency strategy for Iraq. It emphasizes protecting civilians rather than defeating enemies and even uses the term *human security*. It covers such issues as sustainable jobs, access to justice, governance and communication, and the importance of the Afghan role in all this. It deals with "irreconcilables" through isolation rather than direct attack.[22] And already greater emphasis is being placed on creating "population hubs" and "gated communities."

Afghanistan, however, is more demanding because it is more diverse and simply larger than Iraq. There is also the huge difficulty of imposing unity of command and implementing changes of strategy within a sprawling multinational organization. There are two military commands in Afghanistan, Operation Enduring Freedom and the NATO command, which involve many different national commands. There is also a separate civilian effort under UN auspices, not to mention myriad NGOs and private contractors. It will take a long time to shift the enemy-centric strategic culture of most armed forces. What is more, the war is spreading to Pakistan and Central Asia, and it is not yet clear whether Pakistani efforts to clear the Taliban from the border will make things better or worse.

But perhaps the fundamental obstacle to counterinsurgency is the fact that counterinsurgency is not actually human security, however the term is defined. In counterinsurgency, human security, or population security, is a tactic, not a strategy. The end goal is not the security of Afghans or Iraqis—that is a means to an end. The end goal is the defeat of America's enemies, a point that General Petraeus and others frequently repeat. "The fundamental objective in Afghanistan," said General Petraeus at the Munich Security Conference in February 2009, "is to ensure that transnational terrorists are not able to re-establish the sanctuaries they enjoyed prior to 9/11." And among the many items on his list of what has to be done—which includes such instructions as "live alongside the people" ("alongside," not "among," because of Afghan cultural sensibilities), "drink lots of cups of tea," provide basic services, stimulate local economic development, and help establish legitimate forms of governance—is the instruction to "pursue the enemy relentlessly." A human security approach may involve pursuing the enemy, but it would be a means to the end of human security rather than the other way around. Even though McChrystal's report puts much less emphasis on pursuing enemies than did the Iraqi strategy, this is not reflected in the political rhetoric. On the contrary, the emphasis of President Obama, Secretary of State Clinton, or the U.S. Special Representative to Afghanistan and Pakistan, Richard Holbrooke, is on the pursuit of Al-Qaeda.

As we argued in the introduction, this matters both politically and practically. In political terms, a strategic narrative of human security that is actually put into practice would greatly help to garner local support and to increase the coherence of the multinational effort. The narrative has to address not only the insurgency but also the continuing problems of human insecurity that Afghans—especially women—face as a result of the combination of poverty, crime, and human-rights violations. Many Afghans feel they face an unsavory choice between the Taliban, whom they do not want to return to power, and a repressive, corrupt, and ineffective government. What this means is that the problems of governance—of the establishment of trustworthy law-and-order institutions and legitimate sources of livelihood—are much more important than the pursuit of the "enemy." Finding ways to remove the impunity of former commanders and other government officials and to build a relationship between government and civil society are priorities in both Afghanistan and neighboring countries.

The focus on the enemy has meant continuing air strikes, often by unmanned drones called Predators, against suspected Taliban or Al-Qaeda positions, especially in Pakistan. One of the most significant technological changes that has resulted from the wars in Iraq and Afghanistan has been the increased use of robots. U.S. forces had no robots at the time of the invasion of Iraq in 2003. By the end of 2004, there were 150 robots; the numbers increased to 2,400 in 2005, 5,000 in 2006, and 12,000 in 2008.[23] Robots can search for mines and explosives, greatly improve surveillance and reconnaissance, and carry out targeted attacks without risking the lives of American soldiers. They can vary from the expensive Global Hawk, which will replace the U-2 spy plane and can stay in the air for thirty-five hours, to the small Raven, which can be thrown by a soldier like a javelin and stay in the air for ninety minutes. Jeff Hofgard, a Boeing executive, described to Kaldor and Beebe the new toy being developed by his company: it will be the size of a baseball, capable of seeing over walls, and easy to control because it uses "guess what—an Xbox" (a popular video-game console).

Drones, unmanned aerial vehicles, have been widely used to identify and kill insurgents in both Iraq and Afghanistan. This was, for example, how Abu Musab al-Zarqawi was killed. A tip-off from Jordanian intelligence suggested that Zarqawi was increasingly listening to the advice of a certain cleric. U.S. drones followed the cleric twenty-four hours a day, seven days a week, and eventually tailed the cleric to a farmhouse where he was meeting with Zarqawi. According to Peter Singer, "the farmhouse was then taken out by a pinpoint air strike, guided in by lasers and GPS coordinates courtesy of the drone."[24]

Many of the people interviewed for this book expressed great enthusiasm for the use of Predators against Al-Qaeda and Taliban targets. Predators are very light unmanned aerial vehicles that can stay in the air for twenty-four hours; they have two cameras and a laser designator to lock onto targets. They are operated from drone bases in Nevada and other locations in the United States as well as Pakistan and Afghanistan. General Tommy Franks described the Predator as "my most capable sensor in hunting down and killing Al-Qaeda and Taliban leadership" and "critical to our fight."[25] The Predator reportedly has been very efficient in destroying the Al-Qaeda leadership in Pakistan.

Peter Singer of the Brookings Institution, who has written about the growing military use of robots, says that robots are the American answer to suicide bombers. They allow for much more cost-effective attacks. Robots, like suicide bombers, don't have to worry about risking their lives. This raises ethical questions about whether war can be carried on remotely. Even if it is true, and this is not at all clear, that the Predator does not cause civilian casualties, the morality of killing enemies remotely is not only questionable but also highly problematic in political terms. General David Barno, former U.S. commander in Afghanistan and now director of the National Defense University, says, "[W]hen we attack like that in the middle of the night even if we don't kill any civilians we are seen as cowards, hitting from afar in the middle of the night. We should go in there on foot in daylight with Afghan elders and arrest them."[26]

■

The security thinkers around General Petraeus and in the Obama administration prefer the term "Global Counterinsurgency" to the War on Terror. Counterinsurgency, they say, is population-centric; counterterror is enemy-centric. They also use the term *long war.*

For anyone not schooled in the current debates in U.S. military circles, the semantic change seems rather bemusing. For Europeans, for example, *counterterror* means policing and intelligence, while *counterinsurgency* calls to mind the excesses of Vietnam or Algeria. And the term long *war* is reminiscent of Donald Rumsfeld's early description of the War on Terror as a long war that would last fifty years. But the problem is not merely semantic.

At a tactical level, counterinsurgency is, first and foremost, a military doctrine, seen through a military prism. In particular, rules of engagement are determined by the "laws of war" (*jus in bello*) rather than by civil law, which offers guidelines for policemen. Thus, a judgment about whether hitting a military target justifies civilian casualties must be made differently from the same judgment in a domestic or civil context. The war-minded way of thinking is integrated into military units, however much they are drilled in the importance of population security. As long as population security is a tactic rather than a goal or a strategy, the starting point for soldiers will be how to identify targets or disrupt networks rather than the needs of the people. This means they risk deploying force that will escalate the conflict. There may indeed be times when military action has to be used against terrorists or insurgents, putting civilian lives at risk. But this is never the priority under a

human-security approach. Moreover, the starting point for a judgment about when to use lethal force is different; for a human-security approach, the starting point is self-defense or the defense of
a third party. The balance of judgment is, therefore, more likely to
be on the side of saving lives. Even though McChrystal's report
goes a long way in the direction of human security, its implementation is likely to be hampered by the fact that it was his report and
not the report of civilian leaders such as Richard Holbrooke, President Obama's special representative to the area, or Kai Eide, the
UN's special representative.

At a strategic level, counterinsurgency, and indeed "long war,"
remains situated within a framework of "us" and "them." Which is
to say, the equation is framed with twentieth century algebra rather
than a twenty-first century calculus. It is about the conflict between
the West and the global network of Islamic extremists even if it is
no longer framed as the War on Terror. It still appears to have nos-
talgic remnants of the 1945 consensus—something that is perhaps
required for domestic American consumption. A human security
approach is about how to make everyone safe; it dispenses with easy
dualism. When Kaldor asked General Petraeus if the new counterinsurgency doctrine had replaced the traditional war-fighting
roles of the U.S. armed forces, he stated very clearly that counterinsurgency is just one element of the spectrum of conflict and that it
remains important to prepare for major interstate wars. Human security is about a common global effort to make people safe. Of
course, interstate war is perhaps the biggest threat to human security, but the threat lies in the threat of war itself, not a foreign attack;
it is a threat to all human beings, not just to Americans. Traditional
war thinking will always find an echo among competing powers or
in notions of jihad. It legitimizes Russian militarists, Chinese traditionalists, and, of course, angry young Muslim men.

The War on Terror, as it was fought in Iraq and Afghanistan, un-
leashed a complex and lethal twenty-first century phenomenon on
which the global networks of terror feed; it is engulfing many of the
places mentioned by Bush in his War on Terror speeches—the suburbs of European cities, and large parts of Africa and Asia. The situation is actually much more dangerous than it was in 2001—and
in Afghanistan, Pakistan, and Central Asia, not to mention Central
and Eastern Africa—the challenges are mind-boggling. The effort
to produce security using twentieth-century notions has actually
consumed security for the twenty-first century. There is a huge tension in current thinking. On the one hand, the new counterinsurgency tactics are an extraordinary step forward that should in no
way be dismissed. The shift from a mentality of killing to the idea
of population security marks a definitive break with the dominant
assumptions in the U.S. military. On the other hand, the language
of war and counterinsurgency; the continued enthusiasm for technological solutions, as signified by the sinister evolution of combat
robots and Predator drones; and the dominance of military actors—
could easily overturn the gains of "living amongst the people."

So what answer does a human-security narrative offer?

5

"Escorting Kids to Kindergarten": Human Security in Action

Condoleezza Rice, shortly before she was appointed National Security Advisor, succinctly demonstrated her twentieth-century instincts about security when, interviewed by the *New York Times*, she said: "Carrying out civil administration and police functions is simply going to degrade the American capability to do the things America has to do. We don't need to have the 82nd Airborne escorting kids to kindergarten."

New York Times, **October 27, 2000**

Escorting kids to kindergarten is emblematic of human security in action. In zones of insecurity, children may not be able to attend school because they risk being kidnapped or seized to become child soldiers or child prostitutes, because the route to school is rife with fighting or land mines; because their families do not have enough money to pay for books or uniforms; because they have to stay at home and look after their siblings while their mothers work; or because there is no school and there are no teachers. So being able to take kids to kindergarten is a measure of human security.

Studies show that primary education, especially the education of girls, is one of the most important factors contributing to development and stability. Moreover, when members of the 82nd Airborne escort kids safely to school, they gain the trust of the local population, which is the key precondition for all the other tasks of a human-security approach. It is even better if the 82nd Airborne helps local people (military, police, or parents) to escort kids to kindergarten.

So what else has to be done to implement human security, especially in places wracked by violence? The experience of the British Army in Basra, in the Shi'ia-dominated south of Iraq, is a case study of the limits of counterinsurgency and the potential for human security. British forces were responsible for security in Basra from the invasion in March 2003 until their withdrawal in June 2009. In the early days after the invasion, they were rather confident that they could cope because of their long experience in colonial policing and in Northern Ireland. Indeed, the methods they adopted were much the same as those adopted in the surge three years later. The British strongly criticized their American counterparts for their heavy-handed tactics, often causing exasperation. One senior American official said of Major-General Jonathan Shaw, the British commander: "It's insufferable. He comes on and he lectures everybody in the room about how to do a counterinsurgency … the notorious Northern Ireland came up again."[1]

The situation in Basra was initially peaceful. Basrawis welcomed the British with open arms, having suffered greatly under Saddam Hussein. British soldiers were able to patrol the streets and hand out food aid, winning "hearts and minds" and maintaining security largely through deals with local religious and tribal militia leaders. Like Sarajevo and Baghdad, Basra had historically been a wealthy cosmopolitan city with a population that included Muslims, Jews, and Christians (Chaldean, Assyrian, and Armenian), as well as Mandaeans (a pre-Islamic Gnostic sect), Arabs, Kurds, and even a black minority dating from the eighth century. It had suffered greatly from the loss of its date and palm industry after the discovery of oil, and more recently from the war with Iran and UN-imposed sanctions, the brutal treatment of the Marsh Arabs, and Saddam Hussein's total neglect of the city as punishment for the 1991 uprisings against him. The city's population had swelled with poor Shi'ia immigrants after-the draining of the marshes.

Basra's security situation deteriorated dramatically within a short period. Armed Islamist groups made their appearance on the streets of Basra soon after the invasion. In addition to the Badr Corps and the Mahdi army, these groups included Al-Fadhila (a Sadrist spin-off founded in 2003) and Tha'r Allah (a local party formed by Yusif al-Musawi, the leader of the Shaykhiya Muslim minority). It was Islamist groups, dominated by Al-Fadhila, that took over the provincial government after the elections of 2005. Violence began as revenge attacks against former Ba'athist Party members and military officials but graduated into a toxic hybrid of political and criminal activities, including the following:

- Insurgent attacks against British forces, especially by the Mahdi army, which forced the British to take cover and protect themselves, reducing their presence on the streets.
- Sectarian cleansing against Sunnis and Christians. (Some people whom Kaldor interviewed claimed that this was not sectarianism; it was largely because Sunnis were former Ba'athists and Christians were wealthy and could afford to leave.) In particular, the Christians who were licensed to sell alcohol were targeted.
- A scramble for resources among various tribal and religious groups, including vicious competition to control the oil ministry, oil facilities, and the oil workers' trades union so as to siphon off oil revenue.

- Honor killings, killings of prominent intellectuals, and attacks on women who did not wear head scarves.
- Pervasive criminality with rampant kidnapping and hostage taking for ransom. Many of the people whom Kaldor met in Basra had experienced the kidnapping of a family member or someone else close to them. Two of the sons of her local guide had been kidnapped; one escaped and one was ransomed. A woman running an NGO had been kidnapped when seven months pregnant. She was released only when the kidnappers found that it was a case of mistaken identity; they had thought she was someone who worked at the airport for the British.

Included in this lethal brew of politics and crime were demands for an autonomous Shi'ia region in the south. The main proponent of this idea was the Islamic Supreme Council of Iraq (ISCI), a political party that favored a region composed of nine Shi'ia-dominated governorates in the south, while Al-Fadhila favored a region largely concentrated on Basra because it had no base in other regions. Prominent Americans such as Leslie Gelb and Peter Galbraith have supported these demands because they see partition, as in Bosnia and Herzegovina, as a solution to sectarian conflict. As Kaldor was to discover, there is little support for these proposals among ordinary Basrawis who have always considered themselves to be Iraqi. Earlier attempts to carve out an autonomous region have always failed, and, indeed, as the historian Reidar Visser has convincingly shown, there is no historical precedent for such a proposal.[2]

The violence in Basra was nourished by widespread poverty. The paradox of Basra is that despite the fact that it sits on top of one of the richest oil reserves in the world—black oil seeps through the sand—and despite its wealthy past, it has become one of the poorest cities in the world. Infrastructure never kept pace with the explosion of the population, and what little that existed was utterly corroded by years of neglect. The slums in suburbs like Hayyaniya are as deprived as any third-world shantytown. Some 70 to 80 percent of the population of Basra is unemployed. In the slums there is no electricity or running water or access to clean sanitation. Half-built and half-destroyed dwellings, open sewers, mud, and trash litter the gray-and-brown landscape.

As the situation got worse and worse, the British decided in September 2007 that, because they were part of the problem—the target of many attacks—they should withdraw to Basra Airport. At just the moment when the Americans were succeeding in developing a model of counterinsurgency that had many similarities with the early British approaches, the British were abandoning their efforts. They made a deal with the Mahdi army supposedly to reduce violence and to secure their retreat. It was an ignominious moment.

So what went wrong? Part of the answer is that the British were unprepared and thin on the ground. They had been told that the war would be over quickly as a result of the use of "overwhelming force" and that it was unnecessary to prepare for reconstruction. They assumed that they would be welcomed; yet although Basrawis hated Saddam Hussein they were also deeply suspicious of foreign occupiers. A poll taken soon after the invasion showed that 53.7 percent of the people thought that the British were occupiers; this had risen to 75.7 percent of the population by October. As one Supreme Council for the Islamic Revolution in Iraq (SCIRI) political leader said in July 2003: "We told the British that their forces are too small to protect us and people don't respect the ordinary police.... They told us they'd make Iraq an ideal country in the Middle East. They've made it a symbol of looting and destruction."[3]

The British had no idea of the depth and breadth of the problem—the disintegrating infrastructure, the traumatized population, and the collapse of governance. They lacked appropriate equipment for countering roadside bombs, for example, and for operating in the desert. They did not have enough men to "flood" the disturbed areas with patrols as the counterinsurgency strategy recommended. They went into Basra with 40,000 troops but rapidly reduced to 8,000 and most of the time had approximately 4,000 rising to nearly 6,000 in the last few months; at least 33,000 would have been needed to maintain security in a city the size of Basra. They also lacked civilian support. A particular problem was the lax way they recruited in order to quickly build a police force, which allowed for massive militia infiltration. But above all, the British troops lacked political and moral support. Even though many officers had privately opposed the invasion, they were, of course, identified with an unpopular war. There was no consensus in government about how much or what type of support should be provided. A case that was brought against soldiers for abusing Iraqi prisoners under the Human Rights Act further weakened morale. They felt they were there simply because the Americans wanted them, and they saw themselves holding the ring until the time came to withdraw. Most soldiers wanted to get through their mission as quickly as possible, with the least damage.

But another problem was that the counterinsurgency strategy can only bring short-term security. After the 2005 elections, it was very difficult to confront the Islamist groups who were now part of the government. Similar problems could affect the rest of Iraq if the security gains of 2006 and 2007 are not sustained in political and economic terms. In other words, if the government fails to build trust among all Iraqis, if it fails to establish effective law-and-order institutions, provide basic services, and expand the possibilities for legitimate ways of making a living—violence could easily escalate again.

The situation in Basra changed again after March 2008, when, in what was known as the "charge of the knights," the Iraqi army

invaded Basra, backed by American forces, in order to free the city
of militias and criminal gangs. The "charge of the knights" involved fierce fighting and what the Americans call kinetic operations. Missiles were fired into areas where the militias were
thought to reside, killing civilians and militants alike. This was
followed by several months of high-intensity operations, in which
Iraqi units searched whole areas for weapons and arrested suspected militia members. In addition to those held in American
custody in Camp Bucca, the Iraqis themselves detained several
hundred suspects. There were also many deals being made under
the surface. Over a few months, Iraqi security forces reestablished
their monopoly on violence.

The British commander who arrived in Basra in August 2008
decided to adopt a human security–oriented approach, with a focus
on finding the best way for local people to meet their own needs;
he defined the center of gravity of the mission as the optimism of
Basrawis. "The first thing we did," says Major General Andy
Salmon,

> was to become much more embedded than before. It was a con-
> scious decision to embed really deeply. Before us, the military
> transition teams followed the Iraqi army in armored Mastiffs,
> huge vehicles that kept getting left behind especially on narrow
> streets. The Iraqis often got really irritated. So we put the blokes
> in Iraqi army vehicles alongside the Iraqis. It reduced our profile,
> made us less of a target, and it improved situational awareness
> and influence. We used the Mastiffs only for logistical runs at
> night or to escort visitors and reconstruction teams.
>
> Then we did the same with reconstruction. We created joint
> British-Iraqi teams for joint civil-military ops. And we had Iraqis
> accompany visiting businessmen as well. You need to get rid of
> the ego, support the Iraqis and give the operation an Iraqi face.[4]

In the initial phases of the operation, the approach was more military, trying to create zones of normality, free of militias, through a combination of arrests, weapons searches, and local deals. At the same time, efforts were made to improve the performance of the police; some 4,000 police belonging to militias were dismissed. Violence began to dip between September and November. By November, Basra was the quietest it had been since 2003.

But very soon, the British started to introduce compacts to deliver the needs of the people. According to Salmon, "What we tried to do was to get the municipal authorities to get in touch with people and to organize compacts of different sorts. Governance tends to mean bureaucracy, and it's often a huge obstacle to getting things done, especially the bureaucracy left from Saddam's time." Compacts are also a way of dealing with corruption. Salmon says, "Corruption is endemic; everyone does it, everyone wants a cut, and so you can't trust anyone. There's no community social conscience."

Salmon talked about what he called the "index of human security": "Our motto was 'deliver, see, and tell.' It's really important that Iraqis supported by coalition forces deliver something tangible—water, for example, cleaning up trash, or effective policing—and that people see it and they tell others about it. Rumor spreads like wildfire in Basra." The British during this period also tried to create local institutions, like district development forums, so that compacts would be sustainable. "People need to be able to see tangible progress on the things that matter to them," says Salmon. "We allowed them to have a voice and what they want is essential services, freedom of movement, freedom of social ambition—a future for their children."

Of course, key to local institution building is trustworthy government. The provincial elections in January 2009 made an important difference. The key strategy for security during the elections was to talk to all the key players. The British and Iraqi authorities held regular election meetings and used them to focus on constructive politics. They helped establish a set of informal rules among political parties, like not tearing down each others' posters. Everyone expected violence to ramp up, but it didn't. There was a big turnout of voters in Basra (much less in the surrounding countryside, which explains the overall turnout of 48 percent). The Da'wa Party, the party of Prime Minister Maliki, won the largest share of the vote; its members are much more trusted than the previous ruling politicians.

But perhaps the most important aspect of the new approach was the emphasis on respect for the dignity of local people. "The most amazing thing we did," says Salmon, "a massive thing, was to help local people build a shrine in Hayyaniya." The shrine commemorated nineteen local victims of "Chemical Ali," Ali Hassan al-Majid, a first cousin of Saddam Hussein who became notorious for the brutality with which he suppressed internal Iraqi opposition to Saddam. The nineteen people, including women and children, had been made to drink a liter of gasoline before being executed in 1991 after the Shi'ia uprisings. The shrine was built in their memory at a cost of $80,000. "We had nineteen giant candles and all the sheikhs and the only survivor were present at the unveiling ceremony, which I was asked to open," says Salmon. "It was really important because the local people had never felt respected before and it was a kind of closure to a tragic chapter in their history."

Kaldor went to Basra in December 2008. She went independently of the British military and flew in to Basra on a Royal Jordanian flight from Amman. She had been reading Patrick Cockburn's book on Muqtada al-Sadr on the plane. When she arrived, her bags were searched by customs. The book's glossy cover, with Muqtada's picture and English writing, was greeted with excitement by the customs officers, who were probably poor Shi'ia. One of them kissed the picture of Muqtada and asked if he could keep the cover. It was a vivid reminder, right at the outset, of the continuing appeal of Sadrist ideology. At the same time, an interesting dimension of the story was that a British officer was present at customs, yet the Iraqi customs officer showed no fear of displaying his beliefs in front of him.

Downtown Basra felt very safe. Kaldor stayed in a hotel (formerly known by journalists as kidnap hotel) and could walk around and go to a supermarket up to 9 o'clock at night without a head scarf. She walked down the main street and went to a Christian church service on Sunday. She talked to some of the Christians although they were a little nervous. At night, the only sounds were dogs barking, cocks crowing, and the call for prayer. She was told that the Eid celebrations were livelier than they had been in any year since 1990. The only sign of abnormality was the presence of the Iraqi army in the streets.

Kaldor interviewed middle-class people from a range of political parties, from the business sector and civil society, and they all expressed rather similar views. They were all grateful to Prime Minister Maliki for his intervention. The problems faced in Basra, both political and economic, were attributed mainly to poor governance—to corruption, lack of capacity, and sheer criminality among local politicians. While they favored greater autonomy for Basra in the long term, so that Basra can control more of its oil wealth, they believed that Maliki's actions demonstrated the need for centralized government. Many were hopeful that the forthcoming provincial elections would bring in a better class of politicians.

Kaldor had hoped to visit people living in the slums, but her guide refused to enter the districts, fearing, he said, for his life, and not just for hers. The very same day they had this conversation, a British military vehicle was stoned in Hayyaniya. But Kaldor did talk to people who came from there. She was told that within the slums, there are some who blame the Mahdi army, the Sadrist militias, for their troubles, including the loss of life and destruction of homes in the "charge of the knights." But there are also many who believe that the reduction in violence was the result not of the "charge of the knights" but rather of Muqtada al-Sadr's ordering members of the Mahdi army to put down their weapons. As one person who knows them well said chillingly: "If Muqtada gives the order, they will write their wills and kiss their families goodbye."

■

A human-security approach aims at preventing an escalation of violence. In areas of insecurity, there is no clear distinction between war and peace, and there are many possible causes of conflict. They were all present in Basra. There were religious differences (between Sunni, Shi'ia, and Christian communities), ideological differences (opposition to Ba'athism), tribal competition, extreme social and economic inequality, and a scramble for oil revenues. There was also nationalist resistance to foreign occupation. However, conflict is present in all societies, and it can be an opportunity for creativity as well as destruction. Indeed, some theorists argue that conflict is the opposite of violence; violence is a rupture that prevents division and difference.[5] Although conflict is often more polarized in areas of insecurity, the real difference between areas of security and areas of insecurity is the existence of mechanisms for managing conflicts peacefully.

Democracy can be viewed as the peaceful management of conflicts. In the United States, there is a big division between Republicans and Democrats, but no one really imagines that this will lead to civil war, not because the divide is not deep but because there exists a set of institutions—elections, Congress, the legal system, the police, the media, the right to association—to prevent violence, to eliminate private sources of violence (e.g., access to illegal weapons), and to channel conflict into more or less constructive debate and argument. These institutions create a buffer that absorbs the risks of violent conflict.

In areas of insecurity, this buffer do not exist or are very thin. In Basra, the local government had failed to provide basic services over a long period. There had been no elections, and, before the invasion, government positions were packed with Saddam supporters. Although there was a strong police force, the justice system was totally untrustworthy. When the British arrived, they had no capacity to run a government and they allowed partisan people to infiltrate the police. There were unemployed young men with nothing to do. There was plenty of oil money acquired licitly or illicitly to pay them to fight. And there were many conflict entrepreneurs (warlords, paramilitary leaders, criminal gangs) ready to exploit the insecurity and organize the violence for personal and political gain.

When prevention fails, and violence escalates, a human-security approach aims to reverse the process: to stop the violence rather than to side with one party to the violence. This is much more expensive and difficult than prevention. This is why a human-security approach stresses the need to work proactively before conflict turns violent and violence turns to catastrophe.

The tasks to be undertaken can be grouped under four interrelated headings:

Sustainable Security

This requires the establishment of lasting perceptions of safety and stability. It is the tactic or foundation from which all other activities follow. In areas of insecurity, people are most worried about violence; they fear getting killed or captured, losing their homes or families. If people fear for their immediate survival, they will mortgage their tomorrows for survival today—abandoning livelihoods, destroying land on which they depend, turning to unsavory strong-men for protection.

In wars, the key task of a human security approach is the protection of civilians — protecting ordinary people from violence. This is the first principle of human security – it is about human rights and, in particular, the right to life. This is very different from traditional peacekeeping, which aimed at separation of the combatants, and utterly different from war fighting. It is only in recent years that protection of civilians has become part of the language of security. It has become standard to include protection of civilians in United Nations Security Council resolutions authorizing United Nations peacekeeping missions. However, very little has been done in terms of implementation. For most individual nation-states that contribute to the United Nations and other multilateral operations, protection of civilians is not seen as a main goal, although many nations refer to protection, particularly Canada and the UK.[6]

Techniques for civilian protection include the establishment of enclaves and safe havens, humanitarian corridors or lifelines through which aid can be delivered, as well as demobilization and disarmament of militias and other illegal armed groups. In Afghanistan, the McChrystal strategy aims at creating "population hubs," or "gated communities." In counterinsurgency doctrine, the ink-spot theory suggests that safe areas can be created spot by spot, and they will eventually spread. Sometimes it is enough to have areas protected by civilian international personnel — the United Nations compound in East Timor became one such safe haven. Sometimes civilian protection requires robust military action.

In Sierra Leone, United Nations troops were deployed in 1999 with an explicit mandate to disarm militias and protect civilians. But after rebels killed several UN troops and took some 500 hostages, British forces were sent to protect the capital. British troops freed the road between Freetown, and the UN began a much more serious effort to disarm rebels. While both the British and the UN avoided involvement in the conflict they were ready to be ruthless when attacked. When rebels attacked British paratroopers at Lungi-Lol twenty miles from the airport, the British demolished the rebel force and gained a huge psychological advantage. On the other hand, after the West Side Boys, one of the most notorious rebel groups, had taken British soldiers hostage, soldiers tried to arrest the Westside boys rather than shoot them. (The commander of the land forces was Andy Salmon, who was to introduce a human-security approach in Basra.) By January 2002, when the war was declared over, more than 70,000 combatants, including many children and women, had been demobilized.

Since 2005, UN forces in the Congo have tried to act more aggressively, especially in Ituri and the Kivus, in disarming militias and protecting civilians. The UN mission has established a protection framework and set up joint protection working groups. Victoria Holt and Toby Berkman report that military protection activities include

> removal of threats against civilians by a "cordon-and-search operation and/or disarmament of individuals threatening the civilian population," the establishment of buffer zones between combatants" and safe areas "with adequate military protection," utilization of an "area domination" strategy through frequent patrols, overflights, and "mobile temporary operations bases," escorting humanitarian and human rights actors to areas, and evacuating populations out of danger zones.[7]

In particular, the Pakistani brigade in South Kivu has introduced some innovative techniques, partly derived from experiences on the Afghan-Pakistani border. Operation Night Flash organized village defense committees to alert peacekeepers to imminent attacks, reportedly through banging pots and blowing whistles. The EU mission

Operation Artemis was an important turning point. The effort was better prepared, than other missions in the area and included satellite equipment and special forces, as well as medical capacity, and an emphasis, assisted by knowledge of the French language, on bottom-up communication; unfortunately, the mission only lasted a few months.

The Congo mission suffers from not having enough troops and from inadequate training and equipment. It is always difficult to balance inadequate force (e.g., insufficient power to protect civilians in Rwanda, Srebrenica, and, indeed, the Congo) with excessive force that kills, injures, or displaces those who are supposed to be protected. And when there are not enough troops there is a temptation to use force less sparingly.

Protecting people is not sustainable security. Safe havens or enclaves have to provide a basis for more long-term measures to reestablish a monopoly of force and the institutions of law and order. By "monopoly of force," we mean a situation where there are no private armed groups and where only the military and the police are allowed to use force, and then only under very stringent conditions. This is where a human-security approach differs from counterinsurgency. Human-security operations, even in the midst of war, are in support of law and order where law and order is based on human rights. This has profound implications for the rules of engagement. The rules of engagement are shaped by domestic law rather than by the laws of armed conflict. In Basra after January 2008, Coalition troops were operating under Iraqi judicial authority because sovereignty had been handed over to Iraq and this had consequences for tightening the rules of engagement. When operating in support of law and order, soldiers have the right to self-defense and to use force to protect a third party, but there is no concept of "military necessity" that can be used to justify killing enemies or collateral damage. This means trying to arrest members of militias and other irregular forces rather than killing them. This kind of operation is, of course, risky, riskier perhaps than offensive war-fighting operations. In particular, civilian protection comes before force protection in such situations. Soldiers have to act more like firefighters or police officers, risking their lives to save others.

Zones of insecurity usually exist side by side with zones of security or peace. Contemporary wars are extraordinarily patchy or fragmented. During the war in Bosnia and Herzegovina, the town of Tuzla defended itself against Serb and Croat extremists through a combination of police and local volunteers and managed to keep the town out of the war. Towns in Northern Ireland during the troubles did the same thing. The majority of the Iraqi governorates have been peaceful. Outsiders tend to neglect the areas of peace, and that is usually a mistake. This is not just because the vortex of violence has a tendency to spread through displaced people, criminal activities, and extremist ideas. It is also because peaceful areas can be used as a model to show the way for more violent areas. Inclusive ideas and peaceful activities like trade can spread, countering the spread of violence. Neglect of the generally peaceful north in Afghanistan, for example, has been a huge mistake; now the insurgency is spreading there. While protecting people and creating safe enclaves, military forces may need to contribute to efforts to preserve the safer areas that already exist.

In many potential conflict situations, apparently desirable cuts in military spending have actually contributed to violence. It is noteworthy that in the early 1990s, the main conflict zones were in the areas where cuts in military spending by states in those areas had been greatest—Eastern Europe, including the Balkans, and Africa. Redundant soldiers sold their weapons or formed armed militia groups or criminal gangs. The surplus stocks of weapons left over from the Cold War period were a major factor in the spike in wars in the early 1990s. Without extensive programs of integration of former soldiers and conversion of equipment, cuts in military spending can lead to military privatization or simply violent anarchy.

As a result, since the late 1990s terms like *micro-disarmament* and *practical disarmament* have been introduced by the international development community to describe the control of weapons and militias. It has been an intensive learning process. In Sierra Leone, despite the demobilization in the final stages of the war, the United Nations was not very successful in collecting weapons and reintegrating former soldiers up to 2001. The UN Development Programme (UNDP) estimated that only between 1 and 2 percent of weapons had been collected. Reintegration programs designed to give ex-combatants skills failed because the skills (e.g., carpentry) were not matched to demand; further, tool kits were given directly to individuals, many of whom chose to sell them.

The "arms for development" program was introduced by UNDP in 2002 to solve some of these problems. In addition to helping the government of Sierra Leone develop legislation and licensing procedures to control small arms and light weapons, as well as illicit arms trafficking, especially on the borders, the program designed community-based approaches to weapons collection. The idea was that weapons collection would be much more effective if it were community-based rather than individual-based (the individual has an incentive to sell the weapons). In this program, villages were offered a development project of their choosing worth some $18,000 if their village was declared weapons-free by the Sierra Leonean police. Each community was given a metal box in which to collect weapons. The weapons were then divided into those which were unsafe and had to be destroyed and those which were safe and potentially licensable. The box was put into the safekeeping of the village chief or local imam or priest. The village was given a weapons-free certificate, at a ceremony, by the police, on the basis of house-to-house searches. When Kaldor visited Sierra Leone in January 2006, some thirty-two chiefdoms had been declared weapons-free.

Kaldor visited one village in the Tonkolili district that had sur-
rendered 149 weapons, and had chosen to build a soccer stadium.
Everyone in Sierra Leone loves soccer; in the village that Kaldor
visited they were all either Arsenal or Manchester supporters. Since
there was no soccer stadium in the area, they hoped that theirs
would become a moneymaker.

The program helped shift Sierra Leoneans' mentality from the
individualist notion that owning weapons is prestigious to collective
pride in being weapons-free. It also brought the Sierra Leonean police closer to the community. And it established local ownership of
international development programs. Even though the program has
continued, subsequent reports do suggest weaknesses, mainly having to do with the capacity of local communities to manage their
programs. For instance, in Tonkolili when Kaldor visited the walls
of the stadium had been built and nothing else.[8]

Effective policing is critical in reestablishing a monopoly of violence and establishing law and order. In places like Bosnia,
Afghanistan, and Iraq, police forces were often part of the problem.
Vetting police and training them to act in accordance with the law
and in the public interest is vital. In Bosnia, the United Nations
used the international police force to accompany local police and
was able to dismiss police chiefs who failed to arrest suspects or
acted in other partisan and/or corrupt ways.

But demobilization, disarmament, and policing cannot be effective without effective laws and an effective and fair justice system,
including courts, prisons, judges, and magistrates. Transitional justice, involving things such as war-crimes trials and truth-and-recon-
ciliation commissions, is critical in removing any sense of legal
impunity and coming to terms with past tragedies. But everyday justice is also fundamental. In Sierra Leone at the end of the war, there
were only eight magistrates left. In the Makeni district court, the
UNDP supplemented the salaries of two justices of the peace (a re-

tired English teacher and a retired engineer) and a clerk. The court had no water and no generator and was very hot. But, said the magistrate: "We can do without lights but we can't do without justices of the peace or clerks." In some places, it is argued that traditional systems of justice should be encouraged; however, these may be invented traditions (created by various factions who hark back to an invented past) and, in places like Afghanistan, can often be very patriarchal and discriminatory.

There also need to be prisons and rules about detention. If suspects are to be arrested rather than killed, they need to be kept somewhere until they can be tried. The period of detention should not be too long, and attention should be paid to what goes on inside prisons, as prisons are often places where criminals and extremist groups are organized and mobilized.

Finally, the role of the armed forces needs to be rethought. In many countries where violence takes place, armies were modeled on European or American armies and designed for European wars. In practice, they were rarely used in wars against other states and their role was mainly domestic—as a symbol of unity, in the best cases, or as a repressive political force, in the worst. So what are armies for? They are often still important in unifying the population; the army in Lebanon has played this role. They can be used for regional cooperation or for contributions to global peacekeeping. In some cases, as in Basra, they are needed in support of law and order; in others, they may be a mechanism to absorb former fighters.

Sustainable Livelihoods

Sustainable security may be the foundation for all other tasks involved in implementing human security, and yet it is impossible to achieve human security without also establishing sustainable livelihoods. Sustainable livelihoods are also about the first principle of human security. Sustainable security is about civil rights, and sustainable livelihoods are about economic and social rights. In many zones of insecurity, survival is not just about escaping bullets; it is about access to food, clean water, shelter, health care, education, and jobs. A human-security approach is about meeting those needs even in the midst of violence. It is about establishing the basis for a legitimate economy to replace the shadow activities through which people survive only precariously.

In zones of insecurity, before, during, and after violent outbreaks, unemployment is often very high. The economic strategies promoted by international aid donors in the 1980s and 1990s (liberalization, privatization, and stabilization of budgets) were very effective at dismantling inefficient state sectors that could not compete in global markets. But they were much less effective at stimulating new types of economic activity. Before they were wracked by conflict, many now-insecure countries experienced dramatic falls in government spending, public services, and income levels, and big rises in unemployment. Violence and conflict sped up the dismantling of the legitimate economy: industrial facilities were destroyed, trade was cut off, and many people with vital skills and specialties were either killed or forced to leave. Indeed, the gray or black economy that is associated with "new war" was often the only source of economic opportunities.

Humanitarian assistance has increased threefold over the last two decades.[9] It now accounts for between 10 and 20 percent of all official development assistance. Humanitarian assistance can be viewed as a sort of safety net in societies where the normal coping mechanisms have been undermined by the transition from centralized to market economies and by violent upheaval. While humanitarian assistance is essential in situations where people are deprived of everything, it brings particular problems. It can displace local production or pull people away from their sources of livelihood, especially if it is delivered in camps. It is often "taxed" by the warring parties and offers a source of revenue that is recycled into the conflict.

Many post-conflict economies are characterized by high growth rates, largely as a consequence of external assistance. But these growth rates do not necessarily translate into increased employment and self-sustaining economic activity. In very poor countries, sustaining rural production to meet basic needs is key. But in many poor countries, people are forced off their land during violence. These people join the urban unemployed, and, after the conflict ends, many of them do not want to return to backbreaking subsistence farming. In middle-income countries (e.g., the Balkans or Iraq), public works and restructuring state enterprises are the main ways to generate employment. Microcredit (the extension of small loans) has been an important tool for helping victims of war such as displaced people and veterans, especially those who have been disabled by war. But it is rarely substantial enough to contribute in significant ways to employment.

In most "new wars," the foundations of modern existence—electricity, water and sanitation, and garbage collection—are badly damaged. After security has been achieved, reestablishing these foundations is often the biggest priority of people who have been through war. The international community has a very poor record in providing these services—its failure to do so is one of the biggest complaints in Iraq, Kosovo, and Afghanistan. Yet the provision of services can also provide a source of employment. Indeed the failure to provide services can often rekindle violence—something that is explicitly recognized in contemporary counter-insurgency doctrine.

Beyond the restoration of basic services, investment in environmentally friendly energy, communications, and transport projects that use twenty-first-century technology is essential for maintaining and stimulating production, especially in middle-income countries. Integrating infrastructure throughout a region is an important way to prevent the separation and division of communities; it can both generate employment and stimulate reconciliation.

Efforts to generate jobs also need to be paralleled by increased expenditure on education, health, and social services. In many conflict zones, health-care facilities, social safety nets, and educational opportunities have been greatly weakened or are nonexistent. Indeed, most deaths are caused by lack of access to health care and the spread of disease partly as a result of lack of clean water and sanitation. Extremist groups (nationalists or religious fundamentalists) often offer welfare services, particularly schooling, and consequently have a profound ideological influence, especially on young people. Education is key to developing new skills, especially for those affected by conflict such as displaced persons and demobilized combatants, and it is also a way to bring different groups together. Social services reduce insecurity.

Finally, it is important to deal with the impact of the violence on the environment and what that means for people's livelihoods. One of the huge obstacles to rural recovery is the devastation of agricultural land and other natural resources by land mines and unexploded ordnance. Much of the land in southern Lebanon and Gaza is unusable because of land mines and other unexploded devices like cluster munitions. Children and animals are regularly killed by unexpected explosions. By way of example, one of the greatest impediments to Angolan economic recovery, as Beebe witnesses daily, is the fact that rich farmland lies fallow because it is full of land mines and other remnants of the civil war. The cost of living in Luanda is one of the highest in the world—three tomatoes cost nearly $17— in large part because all produce has to be imported.

Sustainable Governance

For security and livelihoods to be sustainable, there has to be a political authority that people trust. This is the second principle of human security. The political authority could be an international authority like the one established in Kosovo after the NATO intervention. Or it could be a municipal or state authority. What went wrong in Basra after 2003 was not just Coalition Forces' failure to help people find legitimate ways of making a living, it was also—most importantly—the weakness and predatory nature of local government. The main reason it is so difficult to reestablish basic services after a conflict is that corruption pervades ruling institutions.

In many zones of insecurity, government is predatory. A position in government is an opportunity to extract resources rather than to contribute to the public good. Criminal/extremist networks that are engaged in violence often reach deep inside government and have an interest in state weakness because it enables their criminal activity. The drug trade in Afghanistan and smuggling in Montenegro are only possible because of state forbearance or, worse, complicity. In Basra, the Al-Fadhila-controlled local government presided over much of the violence and grabbed funds made available for reconstruction.

Among international aid donors and among those who write about insecurity, there is a growing emphasis on state building to counter the state weakness that is associated with insecurity. Indeed, governance activities now account for over half of most Western aid budgets. This usually involves two elements: how to establish formal legitimacy and how to improve the capacity of the state to deliver services. However, both of these elements can easily end up reinforcing the predatory nature of government.

By formal legitimacy, we mean the kind of legal mechanisms through which governments are established. In zones of insecurity, this might be a peace agreement or a United Nations resolution. Peace agreements can rarely provide the basis for long-term peace because they are negotiated not by ordinary citizens but by those engaged in fighting, who often represent the most extreme positions. Agreements like the Oslo Accords (Israel/Palestine), the Dayton

Peace Accords (Bosnia and Herzegovina), the Good Friday Agreement (Northern Ireland), and the Taif Agreement (Lebanon) are often cumbersome, unworkable power-sharing arrangements that guarantee power for those who engaged in violence. If they are sustained despite their unworkability, it is either because of a long-term international presence (as in Bosnia and Herzogovina) or because of popular will for peace (as in Northern Ireland and Lebanon). Peace agreements are cease-fires, not constitutions. They can provide space for a political process that might result in a constitution, but they can also block space.

Another method of establishing formal legitimacy is through elections. But elections that take place in conditions of violence are rarely free or fair. Worse, the expectation of elections may ramp up violence. One of way of exerting political control is through winning elections. Ethnic cleansing in places like Bosnia and Iraq can be viewed as a form of gerrymandering (getting rid of people who might vote against you and packing the area with your own supporters). Of course, elections are important, but only in areas where people are not afraid, where former war criminals are excluded from being candidates, and where public debate can provide a basis for choice.

Some of the same problems apply to well-meaning efforts to improve the capacity of state institutions to deliver services, which is known as capacity building. Capacity building can include programs such as public-service reform, assistance to the judiciary, support for elections and parliamentary procedures, and so on. When a position in government is viewed primarily as a source of personal enrichment and not as a contribution to the provision of public services, the technical capacity-building approach of international agencies ends up exacerbating what is misleadingly described as "corruption" though it is much more deep-rooted and embedded in the very character of the state than this term implies.

Legal mechanisms and capacity-building programs are, of course, important where government has established trust. This is why the kind of compacts described by Salmon in Basra are so important. Government is all about the relationship between the ruler and the ruled. There have to be ways to bring government closer to the citizens so that government responds to local needs. And there has to be a political narrative that provides the basis of trust. By moving into Basra and freeing the city of the militias in the "charge of the knights," Prime Minister Maliki established an Iraqi-nationalist message that supplanted divisive, fear-based sectarian messages. What is needed in zones of conflict is an alternative ideology that can counter religious, ethnic, or tribal exclusivism. This is why the fourth principle — the bottom-up approach is so important.

The town of Tuzla elected a non-nationalist democratic government just before the Bosnian war broke out. Throughout the war, the mayor of Tuzla and the people around him defended "multi-multi" values and developed a historical narrative about the way the people of Tuzla had always resisted imperialism and fascism. It was "like Asterix's village," one person told Kaldor when she visited during the war. The symbol of Tuzla was the goat because, so it was said, when Bosnia was declared a province of the Austro-Hungarian empire, the emperor ordered the people to kill all the goats. The people of Tuzla kept one goat, and it turned out to be so productive that it produced enough milk to make cheese for the whole town. The town's resistance to the Croat Ushtashe regime, which was allied to the Nazis, was also celebrated. The people of Tuzla claim that Tuzla was the largest free city on the continent of Europe in October 1943. A citizens' forum was established early on in the war to promote "multi-multi" values, and during the war, there were many NGOs designed to do things like helping women who had been traumatized by gender-related war crimes or promoting local development and microcredit. Free and independent radio stations, mainly broadcasting popular music, were important in countering the messages of the nationalists.

Tuzla kept production and services going throughout the war, and crime remained low. By the end of the war, Tuzla was providing 60 percent of the tax revenue of the Bosnian government. Tuzla also introduced modern communications and Internet links long before most of the rest of the world. The city was part of the Zamir (peace) network established by the Open Society Institute. At the end of the war, many young people from Tuzla got scholarships to study abroad because they had applied online.

The municipality of Tuzla and its citizens promoted an idea of the public good, a "community social conscience" as opposed to the pursuit of private interest. Education, media, and local associations were all part of this effort. This is what has to be at the heart of a human-security approach.

In many war zones, it is possible to find women's groups, or peace and human-rights groups, who try to advocate nonsectarian values, as was done in Tuzla. These groups are often the first target of violence. They are often dismissed by outsiders as marginal and powerless. Yet even where this is apparently the case, they do represent the kernel of an alternative approach. They can offer guidance to outsiders and, if included in talks, can raise issues that outsiders may not even be aware of. Promoting civil society is, thus, not about establishing and funding artificial NGOs based on Western models, but is key to understanding what is happening, and it is about communication and knowledge and helping to establish a common basis for legitimate governance.

Sustainable Development

The principal demand made by one refugee from violence was not for emergency aid or medicines but for a necktie. "He said that this would enable him to be treated as a human being and not a statue."[10] Sustainable development is the strategic end state that brings together all of the sustainable tasks. At the heart of sustainable development is the dignity of the individual.

Amartya Sen describes sustainable development as the construction of a *network of entitlements* in any given society. These entitlements are ways in which individuals and the communities in which they live can obtain what they need for a dignified life—for instance, production, trade, labor, inheritance, or security (including social security). Thus, sustainable development necessarily depends on and combines sustainable security, sustainable livelihoods, and sustainable governance.

This does not mean that human security is the same as human development, even though development is the end goal of a human-security approach. Human security is, if you like, at the sharp end of development. It is about addressing what Sen calls the "downside risks" that threaten the "vital core" of human beings.[11] Yet, it understands the inextricable links between security, livelihoods and governance. Many of the tasks of a human-security strategy are expressed with a local focus. But human security is also regional and global. This is what the fourth and fifth principles of human security—effective multilateralism and regional focus—aim to address.

"New wars" not only blur the differences between public and private, between prevention and recovery, and indeed between war and peace—they blur the differences between the inside and the outside, and between the domestic and the foreign. The vortex of violence pulls in neighboring areas. Displaced persons, criminal activities, weapons flows, and extremist ideas all spill over borders. This is why any human-security approach has to be regional. If human security is to be sustained in Basra, for example, there has to be a commitment by Basra's neighbors, especially Iran, at the least not to interfere and, at best, to cooperate. The war in Sierra Leone could not have been ended without an end to the war in Liberia since the Sierra Leonean rebels were based in Liberia and the lucrative diamond trade on which they depended went through Liberia, as did weapons. And, of course, the smuggling rings and human trafficking that sustained the Bosnian conflict infected the whole of the Balkans.

"New wars" are global as well as local. Outside militaries, foreign reporters, mercenaries, private security companies, aid agencies, and NGOs are all part of the landscape. And they can be part of the problem. Outsiders cannot contribute to human security unless they are viewed as legitimate. If they are seen as occupiers or colonialists they can easily make things worse. Likewise, outsiders cannot contribute to what is known as security-sector reform (reforming the military, disarmament and demobilization, policing, justice, and the like) if they do not undertake security-sector reform themselves by reshaping the tools needed for a human-security approach. Otherwise they may end up building militaries on the Western model, training new soldiers on the Western model and selling them arms. At the least, this is a huge economic burden; at worst, armies with no external functions can end up as participants in escalating violence.

Human security requires a holistic approach to security, livelihoods, and governance. Creating the tools for implementing human security is thus not only about restructuring the security sector, it involves rethinking civilian programs as well. The key terrain in unstable environments is the human terrain. Starting from a human security standpoint necessarily highlights the interdependencies that exist between security, governance and politics, and social and economic development. It is not possible to create stability unless an holistic approach is adopted.

6

The Anatomy of Human Security

New York City responded to the attacks on September 11, 2001, by calling on firefighters, police officers, and paramedics, all of whom sustained fatalities, as well as the Coast Guard, the Civil Air Patrol, the National Guard, a U.S. Navy hospital ship. Later, the Federal Emergency Management Agency, the Army Corps of Engineers, and the Occupational Safety and Health Administration were involved. The New York City Office of Emergency Management coordinated the city's response to the attacks, and the mayor became the public face of the effort.

A human-security approach requires that the response to human catastrophes anywhere in the world, whether from violent attacks or natural or man-made disasters, is as comprehensive as the one mobilized in Manhattan. In many parts of the world, states lack this combination of services. And in some places where conflicts are taking place, the state may contribute to the catastrophe. What are needed, therefore, are global human-security capabilities that can be deployed at short notice in areas that lack or have inadequate capabilities. There should be a common pool, reserved, trained, and equipped for global operations, and led by people who can secure the trust of the affected population.

Preparation is critical for both military and human security operations. A human-security approach emphasizes prevention, so we need to be able to identify potential security risks and what causes them. To plan, we need new ways of measuring security, new methods of human intelligence, and better forms of communication.

Data

In the twentieth century, threats to security were measured in terms of the military capabilities of potential enemies. Huge efforts were made to measure numbers of men under arms, types of equipment, the scale of defense spending in Communist countries. Publications such as *Military Balance* by the International Institute for Strategic Studies (IISS) would provide lists of capabilities of NATO, the Warsaw Pact, and nonaligned nations. Satellite pictures of tank sheds would enable the CIA, for example, to estimate the number of tanks possessed by the Soviet Union, and hence the threat posed to Western Europe. Many people still prefer this method of counting. A recent publication on the F-22 Raptor, the new stealth fighter aircraft, talks about the "New Deterrence Metrics"; these consist of current Russian and Chinese military capabilities.[1]

There have been many efforts to measure human insecurity or the likelihood of human insecurity. Because this is a new field, the effort is fraught with definitional and empirical difficulties. The Human Security Report, published by Simon Fraser University in Canada,[2] takes what is known as the narrow approach, focusing on insecurity in armed conflicts. The data is produced by the Uppsala Conflict Data Program (UCDP) and was initially based on a twentieth-century notion of conflict. For a conflict to be included in the data, there had to be at least 1,000 battle-related deaths and a state had to be involved. This is highly problematic since formal battles are rare in twenty-first-century conflicts and conflicts usually involve non-state actors or a mixture of state and non-state actors. More recently, UCDP have updated their data to include conflicts involving non-state actors and to include what they call one-sided violence — that is, violence against civilians. In addition, recent versions of the report also include some measure of human-rights violations (in particular, the use of child soldiers). But they still mainly count battle deaths as casualties and provide insufficient information about direct civilian casualties (from violent attacks) and indirect civilian casualties (from lack of access to food and medicine, the spread of disease in conflict zones, and the loss of livelihoods). Moreover, they depend primarily on media reports, which tend to underreport deaths and whose coverage is incomplete.

Other efforts have attempted to quantify an interrelated set of factors that affect the well-being of human beings. Thus, for example, the Arab Human Development Report for 2009 addresses the challenges to human security in the Arab region. It includes qualitative and quantitative data on seven dimensions of human security (taken from the 1994 Human Development Report, which first used the term).[3] These are people and their environment; the state and its insecure people; the vulnerability of those lost from sight (women, children, displaced persons, and the like); volatile growth; high unemployment and persisting poverty; hunger, malnutrition, and food insecurity; and health-security challenges. The report provides invaluable documentation of human-development failings in the Middle East that would undoubtedly need to be studied by those identifying insecurity in the Middle East. But because the report's scope is so broad, there is perhaps an inadequate emphasis on physical threats to security, which are most pressing for people who experience them; these are not only deaths from violent conflict as in Gaza but include the breakdown of or disruptions in law and order.

Indicators need to be developed to address the physical aspect of insecurity. In addition to violent conflict, these include human-rights violations, violent crime, domestic violence, refugees and displaced persons, and casualties from natural disasters (e.g., floods, hurricanes, and earthquakes). A number of organizations collect data on human-rights violations (Human Rights Watch, Freedom House, Amnesty International, the U.S. State Department, the UK's Foreign and Commonwealth Office), but the results tend to be anecdotal and difficult to compare. The major database for crime statistics is a project of the UN Office of Drugs and Crime.[4] It collects data via questionnaires addressed to governments. However, as is typical with these kinds of data, coverage is weakest in those countries experiencing the greatest insecurity. Other sources of information about crime include statistics collected and supplied by national governments. These vary greatly in terms of availability and coverage.

Obtaining comparable data on domestic violence is extremely difficult, for a number of reasons. Definitions vary between sources, and so, therefore, do measurements. Currently there is no central or major database for this indicator. Case studies exist for individual countries, and it is possible to draw information from reports by Amnesty International, Oxfam, local women's groups, and the like, but there is no global repository for "hard figures." Official statistics are scarce, especially in developing countries.

Data on refugees and internally displaced persons is more comprehensive. The United Nations High Commission for Refugees (UNHCR) provides detailed statistics on refugees and internally displaced persons, as does the United States Committee for Refugees. The Internal Displacement Monitoring Centre in Geneva also traces internally displaced people.[5] According to UNHCR's 2008 Global Trends Report, some 42 million people are uprooted worldwide; 16 million are refugees and some 26 million are internally displaced people.[6]

Finally, the main source of information about victims of natural or man-made disasters is the international disaster database at the

University of Louvain in Belgium.[7] A general problem with this data collection, like in any database that builds on various sources, is the dependency on the individual data suppliers and their accuracy. This is especially problematic because the original data is not specifically collected for statistical purposes. In addition, data for a number of countries is not available in the database at all.

What is needed is an international statistical institution that can pull together this miscellaneous collection of facts, fill gaps, and improve accuracy. It is extraordinary that, whereas information about military casualties involving regular forces is accurate and detailed, in most conflicts, even the order of magnitude of civilian casualties is disputed. There needs to be data collection on civilian casualties that depends on the kind of epidemiological methods developed by the World Health Organization for tracing the spread of disease, rather than patchy reports based on media coverage. Moreover, statistics that could assist planners in identifying areas of actual or impending insecurity are, at present, quite inadequate.[8]

Intelligence

During the Cold War, intelligence tended to focus either on technologically driven information, especially satellite photographs, or on the behavior of states and officials rather than society, with an emphasis on potential enemies. This is why, time and time again, the intelligence community was taken by surprise. Three examples illustrate this.

The intelligence community was taken by surprise by the fall of the Shah of Iran in January 1979, and, when in November 1979 sixty-six U.S. citizens and diplomats were taken hostage by an angry mob in Iran, there was little reliable intelligence information to guide what became a failed rescue effort. Similar shortcomings characterized the U.S. Embassy bombing and the Marine barracks bombing in Lebanon in 1983.[9] In both cases there was abundant intelligence based on satellite photos but very little from human sources. As Lieutenant Colonel Donald Anderson, the Marine commander, stated: "the biggest shortcoming [in intelligence was] the inability of the Marines to gauge the feelings and emotions of the local population on the ground."[10]

Yet a third example is the 1989 revolutions and the collapse of the Soviet Union, which, again, took the intelligence community by surprise. In think tanks, universities, and government offices, analysts of the Communist Bloc pored over official documents, many of which were obtained through covert agents of the James Bond variety. They studied the order in which politburo members sat or stood in photographs of May Day parades in order to ascertain their relative importance. They calculated levels of military spending, numbers of soldiers, and types of equipment through calibrated analyses of satellite imagery of military bases. By contrast, peace groups, individual intellectuals, and NGOs who traveled to Communist countries as tourists and talked to dissidents and ordinary people realized that something profound was changing. For about a year, the intelligence community agonized about what went wrong and why they failed to predict these momentous developments.

The wars in Iraq and Afghanistan have also drawn attention to the need for human intelligence. The U.S. effort lacked Arabic, Farsi, and Pashto speakers. There was a huge wall between U.S. personnel and local people, graphically expressed in Iraq by the difference between the so-called green zone (the protected area where international staff were deployed) and the red zone (everywhere else). During the surge, Petraeus's injunction to "live amongst the people" greatly improved human intelligence. But there was also a recognition that intelligence requires social scientists, who understand society, demographics, and culture. The Minerva Initiative launched in April 2008 is a program designed to promote research and improve the relationship between government and defense, on the one hand, and universities, on the other. According to Secretary of Defense Robert Gates:

> Throughout the Cold War, universities were vital centers of new research—often funded by the government—and also new ideas and even new fields of study such as game theory and Kremlinology ... in the last few years, we have learned that the challenges facing the world require much broader conception and application of national power than just military prowess. The government and the Department of Defense need to engage additional intellectual disciplines—such as history, anthropology, sociology, and evolutionary psychology.[11]

One controversial program has been the establishment of human terrain teams (HTTs). HTTs are composed of military personnel, linguists, area studies specialists, and civilian social scientists. They are assigned to a brigade combat team (BCT), and they support the commander with open-source, unclassified sociocultural analysis. Human terrain analysis teams are similar in composition and function to HTTs, but provide support at the division level. They have also developed a database, called the Map-HT Toolkit, which is a combination of hardware and software designed and developed specifically to facilitate research, analysis, storage, archiving, sharing, and other application of sociocultural information relevant to the unit commander's operational decisionmaking processes. Thus, Map-HT Toolkit products include maps showing the spatial distribution of tribes and related social entities; link charts showing power structures and social networks in informal economies; time lines (for example, the time sequence of key religious holidays); visualizations (for example, topographic views of

Iraqi infrastructure); and reports on such issues as the role of ethnicity in Iraqi power sharing.

HTTs were initiated in 2003, when the Pentagon received many complaints from U.S. soldiers that they lacked adequate cultural and political knowledge of Iraq. The Pentagon contacted Montgomery McFate, a Yale anthropologist, who had been advocating the use of anthropologists and other social scientists to improve military strategy and operations. The initial program, launched in 2004, was known as the Cultural Preparation of the Environment (CPE). Subsequently, McFate developed the HTT database, which included detailed information on local populations in Iraq. Together with Steve Fondacaro, a retired special-ops colonel who advocated embedding social scientists with U.S. combat units, McFate founded the HTTs, and prototypes were sent to Iraq and Afghanistan in 2006. The first HTT deployed to Afghanistan in 2007 with the Map-HT Toolkit, version 0.0. The same year, five more teams deployed to Iraq with the Map-HT Toolkit, version 0.5.

The establishment of the HTTs has, however, been greatly criticized. The American Anthropological Association has formally condemned the program on the grounds that it breaches the ethical guidelines of anthropologists and could undermine the trust on which anthropologists' work depends. According to the Network of Concerned Anthropologists:

> During the Vietnam War knowledge generated by the equivalent of Human Terrain Mapping (CORDS) was used in Project Phoenix to target the assassination of thousands of Vietnamese. In Guatemala anthropological research was used by death squads in the selection of victims. The creators of the Human Terrain Team concept have spoken about integrating cultural and tactical intelligence on the battlefield, and Assistant Deputy Under Secretary of Defense, John Wilcox, has said that Human Terrain

Mapping "enables the entire kill chain." Human Terrain Mapping will inevitably be used not just to avert fighting in some instances, but also to select people for death and injury in other cases. We do not believe this is an appropriate use of anthropological knowledge.[12]

Anthropologists and other social scientists face great peril if their knowledge is used to identify enemies to be attacked. The key difference between a human-security operation and, say, a counterinsurgency operation is that in a human-security operation intelligence focuses on human needs and what is required to establish institutions that can provide human security. It may be necessary to identify threats to human security, but this is a secondary function of intelligence. Insofar as these threats can be equated with adversary groups or individual people (as opposed to, for example, hurricanes or floods or hunger), the task is either like conflict regulation (where the aim is to provide a basis for reconciliation among groups) or like police intelligence (where suspects need to be identified for possible arrest).

One of the reasons it is so important that human-security operations are under civilian control is precisely so that social scientists and other advisers can help without compromising their role and future work.

In human-security operations, human intelligence provides the basis for planning. And human intelligence is not focused on enemies but on the needs of the local population. This does not mean that technology is not useful. On the contrary, communications, satellite information, and new methods of data analysis can be invaluable if directed toward human-security goals and combined with bottom-up human intelligence. NGOs, for example, have been using satellite imagery to track human-rights abuses. The U.S. Holocaust Memorial Museum, in partnership with Google Earth, is tracking violence in Darfur by comparing images of villages before and after attacks.[13] Human Rights Watch has used satellites to prove the occurrence of attacks on civilians in the Iraq War and to demonstrate illegal demolition of Palestinian houses in the Gaza Strip.[14] Amnesty International has a project called Eyes on Darfur that uses

> high-resolution satellite imagery to provide unimpeachable evidence of the atrocities being committed in Darfur—enabling action by private citizens, policy makers, and international courts. Eyes On Darfur also breaks new ground in protecting human rights by allowing people around the world to literally "watch over" and protect twelve intact, but highly vulnerable, villages using commercially available satellite imagery.[15]

Amnesty worked closely on the project with the American Association for the Advancement of Science (AAAS), which offered expertise on satellite imagery and other cutting-edge geospatial technologies. Other similar initiatives include the Rome-based INTERSOS project, which has developed a Web-based interactive system, integrating geographic-information-system software to monitor the path of displaced persons to refugee camps as well as the work of the AAAS.[16]

An excellent, high-tech, governmental human security–oriented initiative is the Famine Early Warning Systems Network (FEWS-NET), which tracks food insecurity.[17] It was first developed by United States Agency for International Development (USAID) in 1985. The purpose is to strengthen the ability of governments and regional organizations to manage risk of food insecurity by providing early warning and vulnerability information on emerging food security issues. It works in Africa, Central America, Haiti, Afghanistan, and the United States. Funded by USAID, it is implemented by a private firm, Chemonics International, and several U.S. government agencies, including the United States Geological Survey, NASA, the National Oceanic and Atmospheric Administration, and the USDA.

Where intelligence and intelligence activities of the twentieth century were designed to be compartmentalized to protect against the possibility of penetration by the enemy, the exact opposite is needed for the twenty-first century. These same activities should be transparent, open, and shared with trusted partners. Where twentieth-century intelligence looked at air, land, and ground forces, twenty-first-century intelligence will have to see forces of nature. To date, there's not been much information found about mosquitoes carrying malaria or pending natural disasters that shouldn't be shared among communities of interest.

Communications

Communication is crucial for military operations, but it tends to be top-down and vertically organized, and a great deal of emphasis is placed on secrecy. Two types of communication are critical. One is strategic communication to explain and justify the mission both to the local population and to the public back home. The other is communication among the various components of the mission to direct, coordinate, and keep the various units informed. Both types of communication are tightly controlled, and the second type of communication is highly secretive.

Communication is even more important in human-security operations, but here transparency, openness, and a good interface between civilians and those engaged in operations are key. Communication among the various components of the mission need to be both vertical and horizontal and to be interoperable among different agencies, (civil and military), and different international partners, as well as civilians and victims. Twenty-first century technologies are essential, but in open-source interactions rather than stovepiped, clandestine endeavors, which can prevent rather than foster communication, cutting the military off from other agencies as well as local populations.

Communication with local populations does not take the form of "strategic messaging"—top-down efforts to explain to local populations the purpose of military operations. Rather it has to be two-way, involving a variety of means. This includes dialogue and discussion at the local level in town halls, cafés, or private homes as well as open media, especially radio, but also new media like blogs and social-networking Web sites. It needs to be "bottom-up"; that is to say, it needs to involve communication and dialogue with ordinary people and not just political leaders or warring factions. It also needs to involve civil society—local religious, peace, human-rights, and/or women's groups.

Communication for the purpose of coordination and information needs, above all, to be interoperable and to be effective in remote places. In current operations, this is one of the biggest shortcomings. Reports from the ground in different operations all highlight the in-adequacies of current communication systems.[18] During the Kosovo war, for example, each of the participating nations had significant communications capabilities, but Ptarmigan, the telephone system of the Allied Command Europe Rapid Reaction Corps (ARRC), was unable to interface with most of them. There were also big problems in attempting to communicate with NGOs, most of whom made use of satellite communications. In the end, the most efficient form of communication was Hotmail. According to the chief of the multi-national joint logistics headquarters for the NATO force in Kosovo: "We each deployed with our own communications system, none of which could talk to the other."[19] The best solution for human-security communications is to make use of the best available civilian ca-pabilities—cell phones and the Internet—as well as satellite technology to ensure coverage in remote places.

A fascinating recent example of participatory technology, which makes use of existing civilian technologies in areas of human insecurity is *Ushahidi*. Ushahidi means "testimony" or "witness" in Swahili. Ushahidi was developed during the 2007/2008 electoral violence in Kenya. It combines social-networking technology with Google Maps to share local-level disaster information.[20] It allows any mobile-phone user to report community tension, violence, looting, and other incidents via local SMS messages. The incidents are verified by a local NGO and then displayed on a Web-based map using the Ushahidi Web engine.[21] Kenya was the first testing ground, and now Ushahidi is jumping into other countries in conflict. As of November 2009, the group was already receiving an average of four reports a day from the DRC. This growing breadth could make Ushahidi something like the Wikipedia of conflicts, wrote Harvard researchers Joshua Goldstein and Juliana Rotich in a recent paper: "They are tools that allow cooperation on a massive scale."[22] Al-Jazeera is now using the Ushahidi technology to report on the Gaza conflict.[23]

Personnel

The human-security officer is a new type of hero with a mandate to help humanity. Groups of human-security personnel could be called *engagement brigades*. Each brigade might contain a mix of capabilities ranging from the use of force, the delivery of humanitarian assistance, support for reconciliation in violent situations through responses to natural and manmade disasters including terrorist attacks or the capacity to deal with breakdowns in law and order and to stop looting, rioting or criminal gang warfare. There is a role for the military, but it is an atypical role—in human-security operations, military personnel act more like police, protecting people in conflicts. Engagement brigades could be tailored to mirror the security needs of the population. The mix of civilian and military personnel in engagement brigades could be varied according to the situation. At present, military personnel deployed overseas far exceed civilian personnel. U.S. troops, theoretically available for deployment overseas, number half a million, while the State Department has only 6,000 employees. As of 2008, there were sixty peace operations in the world employing 187,586 personnel, of which 166,146 were military and 21,440 were civilians, including 13,409 police officers.[24] For human-security operations, there would need to be a much higher proportion of civilian personnel.

Civilian agencies often argue that it is important to keep their distance from the military and are reluctant to be involved in civil-military cooperation. In Afghanistan, the military complain that they lack civilian assets and that civilians have not contributed to the reconstruction effort. The provincial reconstruction teams, which were supposed to be about military-civilian cooperation, have not been nearly as successful as hoped because it is almost impossible to do development and reconstruction when the military part of the team is engaged in a shooting war.

Military-civilian cooperation is only really possible within the framework of a human-security mission. Humanitarian agencies quite rightly fear becoming targets if they are aligned with the military. The bombing of the UN compound in Iraq in August 2003, which killed one of the most talented senior UN officials, Sergio Vieira de Mello, impelled a huge rethink among the United Nations and other agencies about their role in conflict and the need to retain their autonomy from the military. It was this kind of reasoning that led the International Red Cross to develop humanitarian principles of impartiality and neutrality in order to preserve what became known as humanitarian space, where it is possible to help victims of war regardless of which side they are on.

The problem is that the concept of humanitarian space depends on a traditional notion of war in which there are two distinct sides who fight each other and who, at least in theory, respect the rules of warfare. In contemporary violent upheavals, humanitarian space no longer exists. The only safe spaces are military bases. And when militaries are engaged in enemy-centric warfare, it is no wonder that civilian agencies feel they cannot operate. In a human-security operation, the job of the military must be to create humanitarian space, to protect the populations and provide safe areas where humanitarian and development efforts, as well as a political process, can happen.

Engagement brigades would constitute a standing professional service available for international human-security operations. The service could be supplemented by volunteers on the model of the Peace Corps, whose volunteers have offered assistance in 139 countries. Sixty percent of Peace Corps volunteers have been women, and, in recent years, the corps has encouraged older people to make their skills and experience available. In the proposed European constitution, it was planned to establish a humanitarian-assistance volunteer force for Europe.

Engagement brigades would need appropriate equipment, especially for communications and transportation. Of course, some equipment will be the same as equipment used in military operations (e.g., light weapons or equipment to counter improvised explosive devices or mines). But in general equipment will need to be lighter, cheaper, and more robust than military equipment, and interoperable by both civilians and military personnel.

It is often argued that equipment designed for war fighting can also be used for human-security operations. "For decades," Secretary of Defense Robert Gates has argued, "the prevailing view is that weapons and units designed for the so-called high end can also be used for the low end. And to some extent that is true."[25] But even

Gates now suggests that increasingly complex and elaborate high-end weapons divert funding away from the specialized equipment and people that are needed for what are known as low-end operations, or what we could call human-security operations.

Training and Exercises

Engagement brigades and volunteers would learn to work together through intensive training and frequent exercises. At present, military and civilian personnel are usually trained at separate institutions. Moreover, military training is overwhelmingly focused on combat in most countries. In the United States, there is a far-reaching effort within the Army and the Marine Corps to shift entrenched attitudes about warfare through the new Counterinsurgency field manual, the Capstone Concept (key ideas for joint operations), and training and exercises. In training, there is much more emphasis on irregular warfare and culture, although the focus is still on identifying enemies. For example, Mojave Viper, a complex scenario-based training, has replaced the U.S. Marine Corps's Combined Armed Exercises. And at the Army's National Training Center at Fort Irwin, the Army conducts training "across a wide range of scenarios from kidnapping and car bombs to reacting to sectarian uprisings and conducting negotiations with village leaders and imams." Nevertheless, combat remains the predominant content of training. As one commentator put it: "The military spends millions to create sites designed to train Soldiers how to kill an enemy in cities. But perhaps equally useful might be smaller home-station sites optimized to teach small units how to cultivate trust and understanding among peoples inside cities."[26] There have also been changes in the curriculum of the U.S. Army Command and General Staff College for the first time since the 1980s, though the emphasis on war fighting, of course, remains.

Exercises and role-playing games tend to be based on past wars; very few of them have been adapted to the new challenges. By reproducing past conflicts, they tend to reinforce traditional attitudes. One of the most quoted remarks of the Iraq War was made by General William Wallace, the V Corps commander in charge of all U.S. Army units in Iraq: "the enemy we're fighting is a bit different from the one we war-gamed against."[27]

There are beginning to be more joint civilian-military exercises. There are some interagency training exercises in the United States. The European Union has pioneered joint civilian-military exercises in its crisis-management exercises. Several European countries undertake civilian-military exercises; the Swedish Armed Forces' VIKING exercises have been made available for European personnel, both military and civilian. There is still very little regular mixed training, although the European Union's Civilian Crisis Management Centre in Finland has been developing pilot human-security training modules and has introduced joint civilian-military courses.

A much more ambitious approach to training, with a particular emphasis on human dignity and respect for local populations, needs to be introduced. Engagement brigades need to live and breathe together with each other and with their local counterparts.

The Private Sector

Since the end of the Cold War, there has been a dramatic increase in the role of the private sector in international operations. This growth has been largely demand-driven. The private sector, composed of two broad groups—nongovernmental organizations (NGOs) and private security contractors (PSCs)—has greatly expanded to meet growing human insecurity around the world.

NGOs are not a new concept, but their proliferation is. During the 1990s, the number of registered international NGOs increased from 10,292 to 13,206, and their memberships increased even more—from 155,000 to 263,000 over the same period.[28] There were various reasons for the growth. One was growing public awareness of crises in different parts of the world and a readiness to donate money or volunteer time. A second reason was the increased tendency for official aid to be channeled through NGOs; this had something to do with the contracting culture and the belief that NGOs were somehow closer to people experiencing insecurity. Thus, by the end of the 1990s, some 5 percent of official aid was channeled through NGOs. In some countries, this was much higher: 85 percent in Sweden and 10 percent in the UK. But perhaps most importantly, NGOs were filling a gap that resulted from the decline in aid budgets and the erosion of social safety nets by structural adjustment programs

NGOs play a very important role in two respects. First, they draw attention to, provide information about, and lobby for appropriate responses to human insecurities in various parts of the world. Human-rights groups like Human Rights Watch and Amnesty International monitor human-rights abuses and put pressure on governments to take action. Think tanks like the International Crisis Group, the Institute for War and Peace Reporting, and the European Stability Initiative prepare reports on crisis situations that greatly improve policymakers' knowledge. Groups like the Helsinki Citizens' Assembly support local civil-society groups and provide a channel for such groups to present their ideas and proposals to policymakers.

Secondly, NGOs offer services that governments and international agencies have been unable to provide. Humanitarian and development NGOs like Oxfam, Save the Children, and Doctors Without Borders focus on material and health needs. Conflict-resolution groups like International Alert and Sant' Egidio (an Italian Catholic group) often provide the basis for future agreements through parallel processes or what is sometimes known as track-two diplomacy. Often NGOs pioneer innovative approaches to problems that are later adopted by official agencies.

There are, however, problems associated with the growing role of NGOs. One is the problem of accountability. Because international NGOs are usually funded by donors in rich countries, they can be more concerned about reporting and proposal writing than they are about their beneficiaries. Alex de Waal claims that at the time of the Rwandan genocide, the main Rwandan human-rights group was busy writing its report to the Ford Foundation. In Afghanistan, Kaldor came across a school built in a place that was accessible for donors to observe although locals thought other locations would be more appropriate. For the same reason, branding is all-important, whatever the local impact. Related to this problem is the "swarming" effect of crises, as NGOs hone in on large-scale funding, which results in considerable inefficiencies, including much duplication, as well as gaps. In Afghanistan, there is layer upon layer of donors, implementing agencies, contractors, and subcontractors, each taking their share of the budget and generating a competitive culture in which the self-interest of each agency comes before the goal of helping Afghans. Kaldor was told of seven layers of oversight in a single project near Herat. In Kapisa, Kaldor was given several examples of excessive cost by the governor, one of the few governors who had not been a commander. According to him, a paved road built by USAID for $250,000 could have been built locally for $40,000. Likewise, the cost of a well built under the United Nations Development Programme's (UNDP) area-based program is $600 if built by a local *shura* (community), $1,000 if built by a local NGO, and $3,000 if built by an international NGO.

A final problem is that not all NGOs are purely humanitarian. In conflict zones in particular, the various warring parties usually establish their own NGOs, giving rise to various terms like GON-GOs (government-organized NGOs) and MANGOs (mafia-associated NGOs). Many nationalist and religious-fundamentalist groups have their own NGOs, which offer a mechanism for mobilizing beneficiaries as fighters or for channelling funds for violent purposes. Al-Qaeda, the Muslim brotherhood, the Christian right, and Hindu, Serb, and Croatian nationalists all have their own charitable wings that organize schools and provide assistance to poor families.

NGOs have a critical role to play in human-security operations, especially in raising global public awareness, supporting and empowering local civil society, and generating a debate about appropriate policies. They are also often needed as service providers, but there needs to be a rebalancing of global public service provision, and those international NGOs that receive public money need to be better integrated into overall civilian-military operations, perhaps through some registration or vetting system.

The difference between PSCs and NGOs is that PSCs are profit-making organizations that focus on the security sector. There is, of course, considerable overlap. Both NGOs and PSCs do de-mining, for example. PSCs differ from individual mercenaries in that they are incorporated and registered businesses, often linked to larger outside financial holdings. Kellogg, Brown and Root was until 2007 a subsidiary of Halliburton. DynCorp has been bought by Veritas Capital, while Military Professional Resources Inc., which recruits retired generals to provide training and advice, is now part of L-3 Communications, and Armorgroup has been taken over by G4S (formerly Group 4 Securicor).

Like NGOs, private security companies have a long history. They have expanded considerably since the end of the Cold War. This is partly a result of the shrinking of military personnel after the end of the Cold War. Former soldiers sought new occupations, and in some cases whole units formed themselves into companies, such as the South African 32nd Reconnaissance Battalion and the Soviet Alpha Special Forces Unit. [29]

But another big reason was the lack of security capabilities in both wars and peacekeeping operations. Sierra Leone hired both a Gurkha unit and the South African company Executive Outcomes at different times to help defeat the rebels and defend the capital Freetown. Ethiopia hired an entire former Soviet air force in its conflict with Eritrea. In the Balkan wars, mercenaries were used by all sides. In the Kosovo war, PSCs were used for the international verification mission, for military logistics, for constructing and operating refugee camps, and even for aerial surveillance. The Congressional Budget Office estimates that the United States spent between $6 billion and $10 billion on the services of private security firms from 2003 to 2007.[30] Moreover, because there is a big disparity in pay, soldiers are very tempted to leave the service and become security contractors. For example, each Blackwater operative costs $1,222 per day, while sergeants in the military generally cost taxpayers between $50,000 and $70,000 per year.[31]

According to one estimate, there were some 265,000 security contractors in Iraq as of Januray 2009[32], of which 55 percent were Iraqi and another 30 percent came from third countries like the Philippines. There were 160,000 U.S. military personnel. Private contractors were officially recognized in the Pentagon's Quadrennial Defense Review (QDR) of 2006 as part of the U.S. military's "Total Force." The 2006 QDR defined the department's total force as "its active and reserve military components, its civil servants, and its *contractors*." (Italics added)[33]

However, the prevalence of private security raises serious questions. For instance, where does responsibility lie when private contractors are used? Perhaps the most notorious example was when four Blackwater (now renamed Xe) security contractors were killed in Fallujah, prompting the U.S. Marine attack on that city in April 2004. Subsequently, Blackwater employees were involved in a number of killings and other incidents, including fatally shooting 17 civilians, among them women and children, in Nisour Square, Baghdad, on September 16, 2007. There have also been accusations that Blackwater employees having been involved in human trafficking involving Nepalese workers and reports about the use of Blackwater employees in covert operations to assassinate Al-Qaeda operatives.[34]

It has been very difficult to call Blackwater employees to account since a 2004 decree, known as Order 17, granted sweeping immunity to private contractors working for the United States in Iraq. Order 17 effectively barred the prosecution of contractors' crimes in domestic Iraqi courts.

Although U.S. soldiers have been prosecuted in U.S. courts for killings and torture in Iraq, the Pentagon does not hold private forces to the same standards. Up to the summer of 2008, no security contractor had been prosecuted. Private security contractors operate in a legal gray zone. Blackwater has resisted attempts to subject its contractors to the Pentagon's Uniform Code of Military Justice, insisting that they are civilians while at the same time claiming immunity from civil litigation, saying that Blackwater employees are part of the United States' "Total Force."[35]

Only after the Nisour Square incident did the U.S. House of Representatives pass a bill that would make all private contractors in Iraq and other combat zones subject to prosecution by U.S. courts but the White House complained that it would overburden the war effort and it was never put to a vote in the Senate.[36] Five Blackwater employees were charged with manslaughter in the Nisour Square shootings, but the case was thrown out by a U.S. District judge on the grounds that the men had given information under duress and that investigators had offered an immunity deal.

Since January 1, 2009, private contractors operating in Iraq have been subject to the Iraqi penal code and Iraqi law on criminal proceedings—even when they are performing under the terms of their U.S. government contracts. Moreover, Iraqi officials may attempt to retroactively enforce this provision and seek to prosecute contractors for acts that were committed prior to 2009.[37]

Blackwater has lost its contract with the U.S. State Department. However, according to a recent *New York Times* article, the Obama administration has retained the services of Xe to carry out drone attacks in Afghanistan in addition to providing security at covert bases there.[38]

Similar problems of accountability relate to other cases; in particular, the charge that private contractors were involved as interrogators and translators in torture cases, most notably at Abu Ghraib. The military investigation into the Abu Ghraib torture case concluded:

"In general, U.S. civilian contractors (Titan Corporation, Californian Analysis Center Incorporated), third country nationals and local contractors do not appear to be properly supervised within the detention facility at Abu Ghraib."[39]

A prevailing concern over the use of private soldiers is one that has always been associated with mercenaries: they have a vested interest in the perpetuation of wars and crises. What do mercenaries do in peacetime? One of the reasons monarchs began to professionalize militaries in the eighteenth century was that mercenaries did not have high ethical standards and they had a tendency to seek unsavory ways of surviving in between wars, using their skills to exploit civilians.

Yet another problem is the military nature of private security companies. PSCs are largely made up of former soldiers who think in military ways. For example, the U.S. State Department proposed sending some 6,000 police trainers to Afghanistan in 2003, but they did not get the funding. Instead, the Pentagon contracted Blackwater, whose excessively militarized training produced "police officers who look more like militia members than ordinary beat cops."[40]

Beebe and Kaldor interviewed Doug Brooks of International Peace Operations (IPO) in March 2009, a trade association representing over fifty private security companies. Brooks argues that the industry is demand-driven because of the huge peacekeeping gap—in other words, because of human insecurity. Even if peacekeepers are available and professional, they lack engineers, logistics capabilities, and other resources. Moreover, unlike military units, PSCs are not rotated in and out. He argues that the industry already performs what he calls humanitarian-security tasks and also that it mainly uses local people as contractors and helps to train them..

Indeed, the growth of the private sector as a whole can be understood as a response to growing insecurity. If public security services are not restructured to meet human security needs, the private sector will go on growing, and this could be very dangerous. It would mark the emergence of a market in violence.

Budgets and Organization

Human-security services could be paid for by reducing and restructuring defense budgets and by increasing expenditure on civilian capabilities. There also needs to be increased expenditure on global challenges like climate change, poverty, and the spread of disease. But our focus in this chapter is how to pay for engagement brigades—or, more broadly, human-security services.

At present, world military expenditures are around $1.3 trillion. Over half of this is accounted for by the United States. The George W. Bush administration presided over a doubling of defense expenditure, *excluding* the supplemental costs of the wars in Iraq and Afghanistan. The War on Terror has provided an opportunity to pro-

cure a range of sophisticated weapons systems that were developed
in the aftermath of the Cold War for Cold War–type contingencies.
These systems are complex, expensive, and less and less useful. Indeed, Defense Secretary Gates has used the term *baroque*. This concept of baroque military technology was developed by Kaldor in the
early 1980's to describe the way in which the defense companies
need to keep producing new systems in order to maintain their capacity and how this leads to the successive development of weapons
platforms that are subject to sharply diminishing returns.[42] Each
dollar spent produces smaller and smaller increases in performance
(protection, speed, accuracy, lethality), with the result that hugely
expensive and elaborate machines are acquired in ever smaller
numbers. These systems invariably cost more and take longer to
build than anticipated; in 2008, for example, the Government Accountability Office estimated that the cost overruns on ninety-five
major defense acquisitions totaled $295 billion, and the average
delay was twenty-one months.[42] Moreover, production of these systems creates a chain of further demands—for spare parts, compati-
ble equipment, logistics, and skills.

During the Bush administration, the number of military personnel
actually shrank, while the additional funds covered new systems like
the F-22 Raptor, a stealth fighter aircraft; missile defense; the Army's
Future Combat System; and the Navy's DDG-1000 Zumwalt-class
destroyer program for open ocean warfare. None of these systems are
appropriate for counterinsurgency or human security.

The proposed $700 billion U.S. defense budget for 2010, which
includes supplemental appropriations for the wars, is roughly the
same size as the Obama administration's entire economic-stimulus
package. By contrast, the U.S. foreign-affairs budget is $40 billion.
And it is estimated that the budget for the global peacekeeping effort
is around 0.55 percent of the U.S. defense budget—that is, roughly
$3.85 billion.

Since 2009 the decline in spending on military personnel has been reversed. What is now needed is a long-term restructuring in which research-and-development budgets are reoriented to civilian and human-security purposes. It is in the research and development phases that big systems are conceived and acquire an often unstoppable momentum.

Much concern has also been expressed in the United States recently about the militarization of civilian capacities. The Pentagon's share of foreign-aid funds increased from 5 percent to 25 percent under the Bush administration. Likewise, the Pentagon has increasingly taken control of dramatically increased intelligence functions. The CIA spends approximately $4 to 5 billion out of a total of $60 billion that is now estimated to be spent on intelligence.[43] According to a 2008 report by the American Academy of Diplomacy,

> the "militarization of diplomacy" is noticeably expanding as DOD (United States Department of Defense) personnel assume public diplomacy and assistance responsibilities that the civilian agencies do not have the trained staff to fill. In the area of security assistance—traditionally the authority of the Secretary of State but implemented largely by the Defense Department—a number of new DOD authorities have been created, reducing the role of the Secretary of State even more in this vital area of foreign policy."[44]

Army regional commands have taken over new civilian responsibilities: the U.S. Northern Command (NORTHCOM) is responsible for disaster management within the United States, while the U.S. Southern Command (SOUTHCOM) and African Command (AFRICOM) have been tasked with tackling poverty, crime, corruption, and environmental issues in Latin America and Africa, respectively.

The provincial reconstruction teams in Afghanistan have been filled by Department of Defense personnel because civilian posts in local government or as expert advisers on local issues or agricultural and business development were not available. Military personnel are able to make use of something called the Commander's Emergency Response Program (CERP), which has funds for quick-impact projects. According to Hillary Clinton,

> I came back [from my trip to Iraq] a believer in the CERP program and advocated for it to continue, but when I contrast that with a development officer or a State Department expert who knows the culture, knows the language, unlike, you know, this very well-meaning and well-trained warrior, and that person can't get $500 to fulfill a development mission that is in service of American security and our national interests, there's a big disconnect.[45]

The lack of civilian capacity is largely due to cutbacks. There was some increase in diplomats under Colin Powell, but these were all absorbed in Iraq and Afghanistan. USAID has suffered a 75 percent reduction in staff numbers since the 1970s.[46] In real terms, it has been reduced by nearly 40 percent since the 1990s. USAID remains primarily a contract-management agency for the State Department. USAID has few technical experts—Clinton recently noted that it only had four engineers for the entire world. To bring the point home even further, Beebe's USAID colleagues often remind him that there are fewer full-time staff employed by USAID than there are members of U.S. Army marching bands.

There have been a number of initiatives aimed at improving interagency cooperation and expanding the civilian component of complex missions. One was the establishment of the Office of the Coordinator for Reconstruction and Stabilization within the State

Department (S/CRS) in 2004. Its role is to coordinate planning for stability operations and to develop civilian response capabilities. The other is the request by the Obama administration to establish a Civilian Response Corps. However, funding is still quite insufficient and the task of the S/CRS is to coordinate, not to lead. The Department of Defense is in charge.

Many other countries are undergoing similar types of restructuring. The UK established a Conflict Prevention Pool in 2001 to finance and coordinate policies on conflict prevention and a Post-Conflict Reconstruction Unit (PCRU) in 2004 that has been renamed the Stabilisation Unit. The prime minister has called for the establishment of a civilian response force. Canada established the Stabilization and Reconstruction Task Force in 2005 within the international-security branch of the Foreign Affairs Department. Germany adopted an action plan on civilian crisis prevention in 2004, while France established the Groupement Interarmées des Actions Civilo-Militaires (GIACM), a strictly military entity that coordinates civilian military activities. France was also the first contributor to the European Gendarmerie Force established in 2004. European states seem to have had more success with civilian-military cooperation than the United States has had.

In the long run, international agencies like the United Nations and regional agencies like the European Union and the African Union should be primarily responsible for conducting human-security operations and should have available standing, professional, human security–oriented emergency-response forces. Individual states, especially the United States, should also possess engagement brigades available to be deployed on multilateral missions. Emergency-response forces could be relatively small, say 10,000 to 20,000 people for each agency. But there could be another million or so in engagement brigades in different countries on standby. At present, there are nearly 200,000 peacekeeping personnel deployed on operations; if one assumes that that number needs to be doubled and that only a third of available forces can be deployed at any one time, then something of the order of a million personnel would be needed. For comparison, the United States has half a million soldiers, while European countries have some 2 million soldiers.

It has been roughly estimated that an international emergency-response force would cost about $2 billion per year.[47] Funding for these core forces could come from the budgets of international agencies, based on either contributions from individual member states or, perhaps in the future, a new family of global taxes on, say, carbon or currency speculation.

Leadership and Legitimacy

Human-security operations have to be civilian-led. This is the sixth and last, but by no means least, of the human security principles. When General Klaus Reinhardt was commander of the NATO force in Kosovo, he deliberately chose to put his forces under the authority of the United Nations special representative to Kosovo, Bernard Kouchner, now France's foreign minister.

The civilian in charge has to have legitimacy. This means both legal legitimacy—he or she must be appointed through a legal procedure and responsible for making sure that the mission operates within the framework of law—and political legitimacy—he or she must be trusted and respected both by the sending nations and organizations and by the local population.

Human-security operations involving military personnel would have to be authorized under a United Nations Security Council resolution. It is not clear what body of law would govern the rules of engagement of the mission—international criminal law, international humanitarian law (the "laws of war"), domestic law of the sending nations, domestic law of the host nations, and so on. This is why the Barcelona Report, which proposed a human-security doc-trine for the European Union, indicated the need for a new legal framework that would provide guidance on what law is applicable when local law breaks down, how to deal with differences in different countries' domestic laws, and how to bring clarity to possible con-flicts between different types of international law, particularly human-rights law and humanitarian law.[48]

In political terms, the person in charge not only has to have so-phisticated diplomatic skills for dealing with the politics of different international agencies and sending nations, he or she also needs to have communications skills to address both the local populations and the wider global public. He or she needs to be a visible pres-ence in the aftermath of disasters, to attend memorials and other ceremonies of significance, to support and encourage new initia-tives, and to mobilize and inspire the human-security services he or she directs. He or she needs to be the public face of the mission so that people can identify with the mission and the mission can command widespread trust.

Above all, the person in charge needs to articulate the political goals of human security in a way that everyone can understand. Many of the obstacles to a twenty-first-century restructuring of se-curity capabilities have to do with a lack of conceptual coherence and the entrenched character of twentieth-century, overly milita-rized perspectives. It is the continued preoccupation with fighting wars and attacking enemies that hampers change.

It can be argued that the current period is much like the early modern period, the seventeenth and eighteenth centuries, when monarchs employed mercenaries and mercenary bands, pirates, and bandits that roamed the sea and land. It is a moment of experimen-tation. But sustainable security has to be provided by a public political authority—a state, a municipality, an international agency, or a combination of all three. Indeed, security is at the heart of the social contract people make with their governments. People trust their governments because they believe their governments keep them safe. Growing insecurity is undermining that trust so that the social contract has to be renegotiated at different levels of governance. In the late eighteenth and nineteenth centuries, at least in Western Europe and North America, governments gradually built up the trust of their populations by building security institutions that protected borders and established internal peace. Now we need engagement brigades who can contribute to human security worldwide.

7

Remnants of the Past and Spoilers of the Future: "Hard" Versus "Soft" Security?

Human security may be viable in Africa or even Afghanistan, but do we not need more traditional approaches in the face of a resurgent Russia or a rising China? Do we require conventional military force to deter adventures like that in Georgia in August 2008 or a possible Chinese invasion of Taiwan? How do we guarantee unfettered access to trade and energy supplies? And what do we do about mad dictators armed with nuclear weapons? Surely we need conventional and nuclear forces—what is known as "hard" security—to address these challenges?

Certainly this is the view of Secretary of Defense Robert Gates and General David Petraeus. General Petraeus told Kaldor that "we still need to be able to do the full spectrum of operations." The operative word for Robert Gates seems to be *balance*. He talks about the need to "rebalance" the Department of Defense's programs "in order to institutionalize and enhance our capabilities to fight the wars we are in today and the scenarios we are most likely to face in the years ahead, while at the same time providing a hedge against other risks and contingencies."[1] And in an article in *Foreign Affairs*, he wrote:

> The strategy strives for balance in three areas: between trying to prevail in current conflicts and preparing for other contingencies, between institutionalizing capabilities such as counterinsurgency and foreign military assistance and maintaining the United States' existing conventional and strategic technological edge against other military forces, and between retaining those cultural traits that have made the U.S. armed forces so successful in the past and shedding those that hamper their ability to do what needs to be done.[2]

Our argument, however, is that human security is more than just an add-on, more than just the "soft" end of national security. It is a way of reframing the so-called "hard" issues—a full paradigm shift. Indeed, the epithets *hard* and *soft* are rather misleading. The paradox is that a human-security approach is often a hard security strategy insofar as it involves the use of force. In contrast, the main purpose of the conventional and nuclear arsenal is soft: it is for deterrence and prestige. These forces are not intended to be used. They are psychological signals—forms of communication—aimed at demonstrating military strength to prevent the use of force by other powers and to underpin political power. But they are very expensive, and even dangerous, signals, and it is not evident that they work.

The argument for hard security depends on the presence of existential foes in the world. So, for Europe and the United States, do such foes in fact exist? Who are they?

In the book *The Return of History and the End of Dreams*, Robert Kagan says that "the world has become normal again."[3] By "normal," he means that competition among sovereign states backed by military power has returned. He argues that there are three major conflicts in the world—one between the great powers (the United

States, the European Union, Russia, China, Japan, and India), one between liberalism and autocracies (e.g., Russia, China, Iran, North Korea, Burma, and Zimbabwe), and one between radical Islam and modern secular ideologies. Of course, it is true that there is competition among the major powers in the world, that many people still live under repressive regimes, and that an extremist global Islamist movement is involved in many conflicts and terrorist incidents. But does this constitute a return to the Cold War or to nineteenth-century imperial rivalry? And is hard power the only way to deal with these challenges?

Russia and China

Both Russia and China are authoritarian regimes, which are typically conservative, defensive, and insecure. But they should not be equated with the closed totalitarian regimes of the Cold War period. Both are much more integrated in the global economy and global communications system than in Communist times, and both have undergone profound transformations.

Russia calls itself a "sovereign democracy." Since the collapse of the Soviet Union, it has maintained a façade of democracy—holding regular elections, for example—while making sure that there is no meaningful alteration in leadership. As one commentator put it, it maintains not "just the monopoly of power but the monopoly of the competition for it."[4] In the 1990s, under Boris Yeltsin, there was much more freedom than there is today, but there was also chaos. When Vladimir Putin came to power, he took control of the energy sector and the media, persecuted opponents, and suppressed Western-type NGOs. For Russia, sovereign democracy implies political independence, military strength, and cultural identity—it refers to "different national paths to democracy" and emphasizes stability and antipopulism.

Russia has become a petro-state. Although this has produced wealth, it also means dependence on global markets. Because it is a petro-state, the regime is more or less independent of society—its revenue comes from energy exports rather than taxes. There is a liberal intelligentsia and, as one liberal told Kaldor, the "government is irrelevant. We just notice them when they stop the traffic in the street." Or, as Stephen Holmes put it: "Those at the top neither exploit nor oppress those at the bottom. They do not even govern them; they simply ignore them."[5]

China, of course, still has a nominally Communist regime, but it has presided over the dramatic growth of a capitalist economy. China is thus deeply interconnected with the rest of the world. This is reflected in a much more cooperative foreign policy and in the growth of spaces within China for debate and discussion both on the Internet and in newly formed associations. Chinese leaders also emphasize the importance of a traditional understanding of sovereignty. Like Russia's, this concept of sovereignty is related to capacity. According to the scholar, Bates Gill, "Those rulers who, through the exercise of *wangdao* (benevolent governance), maintain domestic stability and prosperity while also achieving peace and respect abroad, earn the mantle of sovereign legitimacy."[6]

The transformations of Russia and China are reflected in the evolution of their security policies. In the aftermath of the collapse of the Soviet Union, Russia presided over a dramatic decrease in military spending along with a much greater interest in, and indeed enthusiasm for, a cooperative approach to international problems. The Gorbachev concept of a "common European home" continued to be supported during this period. There were, of course, conflicts, especially in post-Soviet space, and in particular in the Caucasus—Chechnya, Ossetia, Abkhazia, Nagorno Karabakh— where Russia, or parts of the Russian state apparatus, played a role in both fomenting war and negotiating peace.

The rise of Putin led to a return to more traditional security thinking. Military spending has increased. The conflict in Chechnya has been stabilized at considerable human cost. Putin's designated successor, Dmitry Medvedev, has announced a new national-security strategy that will boost the conventional armed and nuclear forces to counter what is viewed as a growing threat from NATO. The new security strategy envisages possible future military conflicts over energy resources and calls for Russia to rely on its own "strength."[7] It portrays the United States as Russia's main rival and throughout the document refers to a "resurgent Russia."[8] According to the document, Russia has overcome the "consequences of the systemic political and socioeconomic crisis of the late 20th century" and has restored its capacity to promote its national interest through "multipolar international relations."[9] This view appeared to be confirmed in the short-lived invasion of Georgia in August 2008, which seemed to intimate a return of traditional threats.

Nevertheless, the security strategy also emphasizes the importance of Russian participation in multilateral organizations. It contains references to so-called nontraditional threats like terrorism, criminality, and religious extremism. And overall, Russia recognizes a version of human security, which is included in the current security concept: "The interests of the individual boil down to the implementation of constitutional rights and freedoms, the insurance of personal security, the raising of the quality and standards of life, as well as the physical, spiritual and intellectual development of the man and citizen."[10] Interestingly, Medvedev used the term *human security* to justify the incursion into South Ossetia. He claimed he was protecting Russian citizens from being attacked by Georgia. Medvedev has also proposed a new European security architecture.

Chinese security policy has also undergone considerable changes since the mid-1990s. Bates Gill has described how China showed much greater interest in security cooperation since the early 1990s, especially in the region. It has been active in the Association of Southeast Asian Nations and the Shanghai Cooperation Organization. It has initiated a range of bilateral partnerships. It has resolved a number of territorial disputes. It has stopped providing assistance to Pakistani and Iranian nuclear programs and has, instead, become interested in nonproliferation. And whereas it supported insurgencies around the world in the name of self-determination, it is now strongly opposed to separatism and what it calls "splittism," bearing in mind its own domestic unrest in Tibet and Xinjiang. The joint declaration of the leaders of the Shanghai Cooperation Organization in 2006 talked about the "Spirit of Shanghai": "The Spirit of Shanghai is, therefore, of critical importance to the international community's pursuit of a new and non-confrontational model of international relations, a model that calls for discarding the Cold War mentality and transcending ideological differences."[11]

Chinese leaders talk about being a "responsible great power" or about the "peaceful rise" of China, even though the term *peaceful rise* has been subject to some debate within China; it is argued that the term *peaceful* might restrict China's options regarding Taiwan, while the term *rise* could be alarming to China's neighbors. President Hu Jintao prefers to speak of peaceful development.

A particularly important political actor is the People's Liberation Army (PLA), which is generally considered conservative and hardline. But even the PLA is said to be changing as a result of exchanges with other militaries through joint exercises and peacekeeping. Some commentators have noted the presence of a "quasi-liberal" discourse within the PLA, one that emphasizes multilateralism, international institutions, and confidence building, but it's a minority view.[12]

By and large, both Russia and China see themselves primarily as traditional powers, despite some less traditional tendencies. This is reflected both in their emphasis on military strength and in their insistence on territorial integrity and respect of sovereignty. Chinese military spending has risen steadily, especially in the mid-2000s, even though it has declined as a share of Gross Domestic Product (GDP), accounting for only 2 percent.[13]

Both Russia and China are rearming; both appear to have engaged in cyber warfare in recent years. China continues to adhere to the "five principles of peaceful coexistence" laid out at Bandung in 1955: mutual respect for sovereignty and territorial integrity; mutual non-aggression; non-interference; equality and mutual benefit; and peaceful coexistence. Russia insists on Principle 1 of the Helsinki Final Act: "the participating states will respect each other's sovereignty. Equality and individuality as well as all the rights inherent in and encompassed by its sovereignty, including, in particular, the right of every state to judicial equality, to territorial integrity, and to freedom and to political independence."

Both countries' insistence on territorial integrity is linked to their failure to respect human rights—that's why they fear interference. They both support regimes, like Sudan, that violate human rights. (There is much Western criticism of Chinese investment in Sudan and other African countires who do not respect human rights). Both Russia and China suppress domestic opposition, often brutally.

The evolution of security policy is, of course, the product of internal factors. But authoritarian leaders are typically obsessive about external threats. Immediately after the end of the Cold War, the Warsaw Pact was dismantled, but NATO did not follow suit. On the contrary, former members of the Warsaw Pact have joined NATO, but Russia has been excluded. The West insists that NATO is not directed against Russia. But NATO is a traditional defensive alliance aimed at defending the borders of its members against traditional foreign enemies, and it is difficult to see who might be the enemy if not Russia. Moreover, the newer members of NATO tend to be rather explicit about their insecurities vis-à-vis Russia. Most recently the color revolutions in Ukraine and Georgia, said by Russia to have been orchestrated by the West, followed by the proposed membership of these two countries in NATO, have been cited as examples of Western hostile intentions. Just as important, at least according to the Russian rhetoric, was perhaps the recognition of Croatia and Slovenia during the dissolution of Yugoslavia, which represented the first revision of borders in Europe after the signing of the Helsinki Final Agreement that was not based on mutual agreement. And the NATO bombing of Yugoslavia during the Kosovo crisis in 1999 without a UN Security Council resolution was claimed to be seen as a demonstration of the West's readiness for the unilateral use of force.

It is impossible, of course, to prove a counterfactual. But in the case of Russia, had the West been ready to put more emphasis on a European security architecture that included Russia, it might have been possible to sustain a much more cooperative, less militaristic policy toward Russia. Indeed, the August 2008 war in Georgia may turn out to be the exception that proves the rule. Ever since the breakup of the Soviet Union, the United States has embarked on a geopolitical competition in the region, which, of course, borders Russia and is deeply interconnected with the instability in the North Caucasus. The area is rich in oil and has been cited in official U.S. documents as a crucial alternative to dependence on the Middle East. American military installations have been placed in Azerbaijan and Georgia, and the Baku-Tbilisi-Ceyhan pipeline was deliberately designed to avoid Russia (and Iran). Moreover, the United States provided considerable military assistance to Georgia, which rapidly increased its military spending, and did nothing to restrain President Saakashvili's increasingly militant behavior in the period preceding the war. At the time of the war, there were some 100 U.S. military specialists assisting the Georgian armed forces. The war began because of a Georgian attack on Tskhinvali, the capital of

South Ossetia; the Russians overresponded, not only repulsing the Georgians but moving into parts of Georgia and allowing irregular forces and "volunteers" to destroy villages and expel the Georgian population. U.S. actions in support of Georgia were cited as a sort of justification by the Russians, and the language they used to describe the invasion was a distorted imitation of Western language. Russia argued that the independence of Abkhazia and Ossetia was no different from the independence of Kosovo.

Indeed, the Western narrative is perhaps the most important influence on Russia and China. It is not just that Western rivalry offers an excuse for militaristic thinking, it is also, paradoxically, that Western behavior offers a model. The language of the War on Terror has been hugely important in justifying Russia's behavior in Chechnya and China's behavior in Tibet and Xingjian—not to mention the way in which the members of the Shanghai Cooperation Organization, mainly Central Asian autocracies in addition to Russia and China, have banded together under the label of the War on Terror to suppress domestic unrest.

Would less emphasis on "hard" power by the United States tempt China to retake Taiwan? China's official policy calls for the peaceful unification with Taiwan under the "one country, two systems" status. However, in 2005, an "Anti-Secession law" was passed, which states that the "state shall employ *non-peaceful means* and other necessary measures to protect China's sovereignty and territorial integrity [Art. 8]" (italics added) should Taiwan Independence forces cause secession from China. Currently, both sides are seeking closer ties, although the "PRC (People's Republic of China) continues to increase, upgrade, and modernize its military forces deployed opposite Taiwan [...]"[14] and Taiwan continues to acquire sophisticated military systems.

Despite the nationalist and militaristic rhetoric from the mainland, most commentators think that incorporation of Taiwan into China by military means seems unlikely. It is not clear whether the threat of military intervention by the United States is what deters such an adventure or whether, on the contrary, it is the threat that spurs militant language. But it is clear that such a move would disrupt Beijing's growing emphasis on a peaceful international environment needed for economic development.

To say that Russia and China tend toward rather traditional geopolitical thinking does not mean that the West has to mimic their behavior. Indeed, one could go further and argue that military competition actually strengthens the hard-liners and prevents any dialogue about some of the most serious issues. What is striking is how little the West is concerned about the massive human-rights violations in Chechnya, Tibet, and Xingjian compared with, say, the Balkans and Africa. The West is much more concerned about the potential threat posed by Russia and China to the West than it is about the threats posed by those regimes to their citizens. Yet it is precisely because of their domestic fears that Chinese and Russian leaders are so fearful about outside interference. The problem with trying to match or overmatch military forces and emphasizing deterrence is that it offers a form of legitimation to Chinese and Russian military leaders.

A more cooperative, less militarized approach would, at best, remove insecurities, build on the nontraditional elements of security that are contained in both countries' official security policies, strengthen those within both regimes who favor more cooperative approaches, and help to create space for internal change. At least it would remove some of the legitimation for the use of military force.

Iran and North Korea

Iran and North Korea were both included by President George W. Bush in his "axis of evil" speech in 2002. Both seem intent on acquiring nuclear weapons, although Iran claims that its program of uranium enrichment and plutonium reprocessing is intended for peaceful purposes. And both were on the U.S. State Department's list of states that sponsor terrorism, although North Korea was removed in 2008. Iran provides financial and military support to Hezbollah in Lebanon and Hamas in Israel as well as Shi'ia militia in Iraq. North Korea was added to the list after the destruction of Korean Air Flight 858 by North Korean agents in 1987, though there has been no evidence of state-sponsored terrorism since then.

But are military threats and economic sanctions a counter to this behavior? How do they prevent the acquisition of nuclear weapons or the sponsorship of terrorism? And are there alternative approaches?

The two regimes are very different. The Iranian regime is unlike any other illiberal regime. It has a dual structure in which more or less "normal" democratic institutions (e.g., an elected president and parliament) are overseen by a range of religious institutions. This is known as *velayat-e fiqh* (religious supervision). The revolution of 1979 involved a combination of leftists and Islamists who shared an anti-Western, anti-imperialist, and collectivist ideology. Hard-line Islamists consolidated their hold over the system in the years immediately following the revolution, especially as a consequence of the war with Iraq (1980 to 1988), which involved huge casualties and economic hardship.

State-sponsored violence diminished after the death of the Supreme Leader Ayatollah Khomeini and the election of Akbar Hashemi Rafsanjani in 1989 as president. Eight years later, the sweeping victory of Mohammad Khatami in the 1997 presidential elections, followed by the victory of reformists in the 2000 parliamentary elections, ushered in a "Tehran Spring," with talk of civil society, rule of law, and "dialogue of civilizations." However, the religious authorities began to crack down again; thousands of reformist candidates were disqualified in the parliamentary elections of 2004 and the presidential elections of 2005, and hundreds of laws passed by the reformist parliament were annulled.

The victory of the hard-liner Mahmoud Ahmadinejad in 2005 led to a wave of arrests, executions (including young people under the age of eighteen), and closures of free media and civil-society spaces. In June 2009, huge protests about what was seen as the fraudulent reelection of Ahmadinejad were ruthlessly suppressed and, at the time of writing, the struggle between reformers and hard-liners is continuing on the streets.

Iran has one of the liveliest civil societies in the Middle East. There are around 8,000 NGOs and associations, mainly concerned with humanitarian issues like drug addiction and trafficking in women. The Bam earthquake in 2003 led to unprecedented grass-roots mobilization. A vibrant women's movement, which started to develop during the 1990s, brings together both Islamic and secular, rich and poor, women. This movement has succeeded in reversing some laws, such as the rules on divorce, and introducing new laws, such as prohibiting stoning.

Although Ahmadinejad cracked down on media spaces, the Internet is a hugely important public space. By 2001 there were some 1,500 Internet cafés, and there are now between 70,000 and 100,000 bloggers. Some 7.5 million Iranians are estimated to surf the 'net—more, as a proportion of the population, than in any other Middle Eastern country except Israel. There are formal regulations controlling the use of the Internet, but they are not enforced effectively, even though Ahmadinejad has closed down some 450 Internet cafés and arrested many bloggers. The government lacks expertise; the Internet is largely provided by commercial providers; and the government itself uses the Internet to propagate its own Islamic discourse. According to several clerics, the Internet is a "gift to spread the word of the prophet."[15]

But civil society in Iran does not only include reformist tendencies; it is also composed of conservative, pro-government, and radical Islamist groups. Pro-government groups include Ansar-e Hezbollah, Muslim Students Following the Imam, and the Tehran Militant Clergy Association. Some groups are more extreme than the government. For example, in January 2007, the government closed down a fundamentalist Web site, which had accused Ahmadinejad of betraying the revolution because he watched a female dance show at the Asian Games in Qatar.

It became clear during the 2009 protests that the country is deeply polarized between largely middle-class and urban supporters of liberal reform and the supporters of the president, who tend to be very poor and based in the countryside. Even though it is likely that Ahmadinejad lost the elections, he nevertheless won a substantial share of the vote.

In contrast to Iran, North Korea, known as the "hermit kingdom," is probably the last bastion of totalitarian communism. It is one of the most heavily militarized societies in the world; the army, according to the U.S. State Department, numbers some 1.2 million and is the fifth largest in the world. It is also one of the poorest countries in the world—millions died in the famine of the mid-1990s, known as the "arduous march," and malnutrition persists. Arbitrary arrest, detention, and torture are widespread. The government runs huge prison camps where hundreds of thousands of citizens, including children, are enslaved. It also holds public executions where individuals are executed for stealing state property, hoarding food, and other "anti-socialist" crimes.

But even North Korea has changed since the 1950s and 1960s, when the Great Leader Kim Il-sung propagated a reign of terror and a cult of personality. Kim's son, Kim Jong-Il, who succeeded his father in 1994, still rules in a personalistic, secretive, centralized way, but some commentators argue that the system of governance in North Korea today involves a degree of institutional competition between the ruling Workers' Party, the military, the cabinet, and the security apparatus.[16] More importantly, perhaps, in the aftermath of the famine, the government could no longer maintain control. It could not stop people from fleeing from the cities to the countryside to look for food or fleeing across the border to China, because the police and other officials had also fled. It could not stop illegal businesses from which officials take a cut. Nor could it control the spread of illegal CDs and DVDs, and even mobile phones, from South Korea.[17] North Korea remains dependent on food aid from South Korea, Japan, China, and even the United States. This dysfunctional regime cannot survive, but whether it will collapse dangerously, with military elements using force to retain their power, or peacefully unify with South Korea remains a crucial unanswered question.

It can be argued that the main effect of military threats and sanctions in both Iran and North Korea is to strengthen hard-liners. In Iran, this began with the West's support for Iraq in the long and bloody Iran-Iraq War, which greatly strengthened the position of the Islamists. During the 1990s, President Clinton pursued an aggressive containment policy in order to isolate Iran. He issued across-the-board sanctions on Iran in 1995 (due to pressure from a Republican-dominated Congress). There was some moderation of this policy after 2000. Secretary of State Madeleine Albright in March of that year announced the easing of certain sanctions and called for people-to-people exchanges. She also offered open dialogue without conditions. However, Iran did not respond to the American offer and insisted on the complete lifting of sanctions prior to dialogue.

After 9/11, there was a real opportunity for rapprochement with Iran, which could have helped the reformist movement. Candlelit vigils were held in Tehran for the victims of 9/11, and in Iran's football stadium, some 60,000 spectators respected a minute's silence for the victims of 9/11. The Iranian government supported the United States initially in its war against the Taliban and helped to establish the new Afghan government. There was some shock, therefore, when Iran was included as part of the "axis of evil."

In May 2003, the Iranian government sent a letter to the American government, based, according to Iranian diplomats, on a set of talking points proposed by American intermediaries. In the letter, Iran offered complete openness about its nuclear program, help toward stabilizing Iraq, an end to support for Palestinians, and help in disarming Hezbollah, in exchange for a halt in hostile American behavior and a statement that Iran does not belong to the "axis of evil." The letter was ignored; hard-liners within the U.S. administration said, "We don't talk to evil."[18]

In a 2007 statement before the U.S. House of Representatives' subcommittee on government oversight and reform, Hillary Mann Leverett, who served on the National Security Council in the Bush administration, said:

> From an Iranian perspective, this record shows that Washington will take what it can get from talking to Iran on specific issues but it is not prepared for real rapprochement. From an American perspective, I believe that this record indicates that the Bush administration cavalierly rejected multiple and significant opportunities to put U.S.-Iranian relations on a fundamentally more positive and constructive trajectory.[19]

President Obama came to power committed to greater engagement with Iran, but the repression of protests following the June 2009 elections, the revelation of a previously undisclosed Iranian nuclear facility at Qom in September 2009, and the testing of long-range missiles that same month have led to renewed calls for sanctions.

Yet aggressive policies do not seem to work. Zakaria Fareed argues that military strikes against Iran, by the United States or by Israel, would be "utterly counter-productive. Such a move would do limited damage to Iran's nuclear facilities, rally the country round the regime, isolate the United States further in the world and probably prompt the Iranians to retaliate by sponsoring terror attacks."[20] In the case of a military invasion, as in Iraq, the result would be even worse, mobilizing the country in a resistance movement united under an Islamist banner and resulting in an even longer war along the lines of Afghanistan. And if the actual use of military force would be counterproductive, then military threats either lack credibility or could drag those who issue them into an impossible situation.

The United States has never really tried to engage with Iran and has continuously pursued a strategy of sanctions and isolation. According to the Iran Nuclear Policy Group of the American Foreign Policy Project, "through endless repetition the myth has taken hold in some quarters that nuclear diplomacy with Iran has been tried and failed, leaving no recourse but threats and sanctions."[21]

Sanctions also appear to be counterproductive, since the regime can use the sanctions to explain the current deep recession, as Iraq did before the fall of Saddam Hussein. Iran's rationing system would ensure that the military and the elites would receive gasoline while the poor and middle classes would suffer; it would be easy enough for the Iranian government to put the blame on the United States just as Saddam Hussein did in Iraq.

According to Djavad Salehi-Isfahani at the Brookings Institution:

The sizeable majority of Iran's economically disadvantaged population that supports the Ahmadinejad government is not poor in the sense of lacking food and shelter. Its support for the current government signifies a clear choice between a populist leader with oil money to distribute and his liberal opponents, who criticize his redistributive policies for being inflationary and dismiss them as mere charity. In this political atmosphere sanctions are likely to cement the authoritarian pact between the conservatives and the economic underclass and at the same time weaken the voices calling for greater social, political and economic freedom. … The sanctions on gasoline imports under review may be a godsend for President Ahmadinejad, who would use the sanctions as an excuse to raise gasoline prices to the middle class and use the proceeds to expand his popular base.[22]

Most Iranian dissidents take the view that American policy helps to strengthen the hard-liners in government and vice versa; Bush and Ahmadinejad were seen as mutually supporting each other.

The regime's greatest strength has been its claim to be the only country in the Middle East standing up to the United States. The nuclear question, particularly the way it has been spun in Tehran, has permitted the regime to emerge as the champion of Iran's sovereign rights, even in the eyes of many Iranians who despise their leaders.[23]

Indeed, it can be argued that hard-line policies have made uranium enrichment an ongoing symbol of Iran's independence. "Across the length and breadth of Iranian society—from reformers to hardliners—enrichment has become for Iranians a matter of national entitlement and a source of pride in technological advancement not unlike our own moon landing."[24]

The best hope for solving the nuclear problem would be regime change in Iran. It would be paradoxical if the West gave the impression that the nuclear issue (the potential threat to the West or to Israel) was more important than the ongoing threats to ordinary Iranians every day. And, if by so doing, it helped the very people who are using repressive measures to prevent change.

The same sort of argument can be applied to North Korea, only to a more extreme degree. The threat of military conflict has been ever present since the end of the Korean War (1950 to 1953). Indeed, the Korean peninsula can be regarded as the last remnant of the Cold War, as massive military forces confront each other on either side of the demilitarized zone. The United States Pacific Command maintains tight surveillance over North Korean military activities and has developed numerous plans and contingencies for possible attacks. It could be viewed as part of a mutual imaginary confrontation in which both sides, North Korea and the United States, are locked.

In 1994, North Korea gave notice that it was about to withdraw from the nuclear nonproliferation treaty but was persuaded to freeze its nuclear program and "suspend" its withdrawal. In 2002, evidence surfaced that North Korea was violating this agreement; the following year, North Korea formally withdrew from the treaty after expelling inspectors from the International Atomic Energy Agency. Despite six-party talks convened by China, which included the United States, North Korea's nuclear program seems to have been continued. The talks seemed close to getting somewhere in 2005, but in 2006, North Korea refused to return to the talks after the United States imposed financial sanctions.

In October 2006, North Korea undertook its first nuclear test. In a statement, the North Korean government said, "The Iraqi war teaches a lesson that in order to prevent a war and defend the security of a country and the sovereignty of a nation, it is necessary to have a powerful physical deterrent."[25] In April 2009, North Korea successfully tested a medium-range ballistic missile, and in May 2009, it announced that it had successfully conducted a second nuclear test. The United Nations Security Council unanimously passed a resolution on June 12 to tighten sanctions targeting North Korea's nuclear and missile-development programs; it encouraged United Nations members to inspect cargo vessels and airplanes suspected of carrying weapons and other military materiel. The United

States and allies like Japan and South Korea have brought back measures, such as freezing North Korea's overseas bank accounts, to which the regime strongly objected in the past.

In response, North Korea threatened a "powerful military strike." According to the official statement: "We consider this a declaration of war against us. Any hostile act against our peaceful vessels, including search and seizure, will be considered an unpardonable infringement on our sovereignty, and we will immediately respond with a powerful military strike." The statement also said that North Koreans "no longer feel bound by the armistice" that ended the fighting in the Korean War.[26]

In addition to military pressure, the United States has also imposed sanctions on North Korea. The problem with sanctions is that the countries that have the most leverage over North Korea, China and South Korea, are skeptical about their utility. According to Sheila Smith at the Council on Foreign Relations

> The Chinese position has been that to really push the North Koreans up against the wall, to harm them or to cut them out completely—of any kind of fuel oil or food aid—would have devastating consequences and would in fact push the North Koreans in the opposite direction. . . . The South Koreans themselves have felt that engagement has had a better chance of influencing North Korea than a more punitive sanctions kind of approach.[27]

It can be argued that the situation in North Korea is desperate—an ailing president presides over a cruel and increasingly chaotic impoverished society. We do not actually know what is happening inside North Korea, despite former president Clinton's August 2009 visit to rescue two American journalists. It may be that the mad acts and statements of recent months are the last-ditch efforts of a regime on the verge of collapse—a moment when military provocation, far from acting as a deterrent, could be very dangerous.

In general, our argument is that hard power does not work when dealing with unpredictable dictators. It strengthens hard-liners, unites the population around anti-Western sentiments, and provides an incentive to acquire nuclear weapons—to deter attack. Sanctions and isolation may work sometimes, but they do not seem to have worked in these two cases. That's why we need an alternative.

Reframing the "Hard" Issues

A human-security strategy is concerned not only with human rights and democracy but also with not using force in ways that violate human rights. Part of the problem is that what is viewed as acceptable in war is not the same as what is viewed as acceptable in peacetime. While Israeli armed forces do try to minimize civilian casualties when they strike what they regard as military targets in retaliation for deliberate attacks by Palestinians on Israeli civilians, they cannot avoid what is euphemistically known as collateral damage. The consequence is that many more Palestinian civilians, including children, have been killed by Israeli forces than Israeli civilians have been killed by Palestinian attacks. But while the killing of Palestinian civilians is viewed in Palestine as a violation of human rights, it is viewed in Israel and often by the wider international community as an unfortunate side effect of necessary military operations. Because Israeli soldiers wear uniforms and aim at military targets, they are judged in terms of the rules of war. But Palestinians who attack Israelis are not agents of the state and are therefore regarded as terrorists. A human-security approach to the Israel-Palestine conflict would focus not on the state security of Israel but on the human security of both Israelis and Palestinians and would oppose both terrorism and collateral damage. There may well have to be defensive operations aimed at protecting civilians, but they would operate under human-rights rules rather than the rules of war.

A human-security approach takes as its starting point the goal of saving human lives, whether they be Russian, Chinese, Iranian, Korean, Sudanese, Zimbabwean, British, or American.

So-called hard power is associated with the notion of sovereignty and the defense of borders. By the end of the 1990s, however, long-held assumptions were beginning to change. The genocide in Rwanda and the massacre at Srebrenica were among the events that contributed to what appeared to be a growing consensus that sovereignty was no longer absolute and that it was conditional on respect for human rights.

But is intervention justified to secure human rights of an oppressed community? And if so, what kind of intervention? Both the NATO bombing of Yugoslavia and the Russian intervention in Ossetia were described as humanitarian interventions, or, in the Russian case, as motivated by a "responsibility to protect." But were they? Neither operation was authorized by the United Nations Security Council, but it can be argued that international law has not yet caught up with changing international norms. The question is, do these interventions correspond with a new norm of humanitarian intervention or "responsibility to protect"?

The NATO intervention was intended to prevent massive human-rights violations against Kosovar Albanians by Yugoslav forces. But the method chosen, as we described in Chapter 3, was diplomacy backed by bombing. Bombing could not protect Kosovar Albanians on the ground. It directly resulted in 1,400 civilian deaths in Yugoslavia, including some deaths of fleeing Kosovar refugees. It is true that the Kosovars who were expelled by Serb forces and who survived the war were eventually able to return to their homes (some 10,000 Kosovars lost their lives), but bombing could not prevent reverse ethnic cleansing of Serbs. The war could be justified for the sake of the Kosovar Albanians, with many qualifications, but it cannot be described as a "humanitarian" intervention, because bombing and ethnic partitioning are inimical to human rights.

The Russians justified their intervention in Ossetia in terms of the "allegedly ongoing genocide" of Ossetians. They also claimed they were protecting Russian citizens. Those Russian citizens were actually Ossetians who had been given Russian passports. According to the official EU fact-finding mission, this "passportisation" of what were still Georgian citizens "runs against the principles of good neighbourliness and constitutes an open challenge to Georgian sovereignty and an interference in the internal affairs of Georgia."[28] In any case, the disproportionate Russian response to the Georgian attack on Tskhinvali went well beyond the protection of civilians and involved setting up military positions deep inside Georgian territory. Moreover, the EU fact-finding mission records many violations of international humanitarian law and human rights, especially by irregular South Ossetian forces, which the Russians did nothing to restrain. These forces engaged in ethnic cleansing against ethnic Georgians and "systematic looting and destruction of ethnic Georgian villages." Altogether some 850 people, most of them civilians, lost their lives, and some 135,000 people were displaced—of these, about 35,000 cannot return to their homes.

A humanitarian intervention is not the same as war. A humanitarian intervention has to be focused on the protection of civilians and cannot kill the very people it is supposed to protect. In the case of the Kosovo war, the aim was humanitarian but the means of war were highly problematic. In the case of Ossetia, it is less clear whether the aim was humanitarian or had to do with a growing geopolitical conflict with Georgia, but even if Russian statements are taken at face value, it cannot be described as a humanitarian intervention since it was not focused on the protection of civilians.

A humanitarian intervention on human-rights grounds must be carried out according to the principles of human security. This is not a question of semantics: unless the principles of human security are fully appreciated, the language will be misapplied, even claimed by those wishing to use human security as a cloak for something else.

If sovereignty is conditional on respect for human rights, is there a case for revision of borders when the collective rights of peoples are violated? This concept of self-determination was the argument used to free colonial peoples from European rule. Does it also apply to Kosovars, Ossetians, Tibetans, Uighurs, Chechens? And are all these cases the same?

Kaldor first visited South Ossetia in the summer of 1995. She was ushered in to meet the so-called foreign minister of the enclave. To her surprise, a large portrait of Radovan Karadzic, the Bosnian Serb war criminal brought to trial in The Hague in 2009, was prominently displayed on the wall. When she asked him about it, he said that the portrait had been presented to him by the Bosnian Serb delegation at a meeting of Eastern Christians and that he greatly admired the Bosnian Serbs' stance on independence.

The story is revealing because it suggests that the Balkan parallel with Ossetia (and Abkhazia) is not Kosovo, as the Russians claim, but Republika Srpska. Republika Srpska is a Serb-dominated separate "entity" within Bosnia and Herzegovina. It was established during the war through expelling Muslims and Croats. Ossetia and Abkhazia, two breakaway statelets, originally provinces within the Soviet republic of Georgia, were created with Russian support during the breakup of the Soviet Union—probably as a way of maintaining control over the South Caucasus, which Russian traditionalists regard as their sphere of influence. At that time, of course, the Russian state was not unified, and so whether this was deliberate policy or part of the jockeying for power among sections of the military, remnants of the KGB, and Russian mafia who want to control Black Sea tourism will never be known.

Both enclaves are isolated, underpopulated, and characterized by fear, lawlessness, and poverty, which exacerbate ethnic polarization and criminality.

The debate about the future of South Ossetia (and Abkhazia) is rarely framed in human terms, but instead in terms of status issues and geopolitics, the principle of territorial integrity versus the principle of self-determination. But this serves only to harden the conflict. When the debate is framed in human-security terms, different outcomes are possible. Does it matter whether Northern Ireland is part of Ireland, part of Britain, or part of Timbuctoo as long as Catholics and Protestants can live alongside each other in their own homes? Did it matter whether Yugoslavia remained one state or became six states (the six republics) or eight states (the six republics plus two autonomous provinces) or more, as long as individuals could live in their communities without fear of violence? In other words, the solution to the question of status should be secondary to the principle of human rights.

There is a strong case for the independence of Kosovo because there are good reasons to fear for the human rights of Kosovar Albanians, based on past experience, should the province be returned to Serbia. At the same time, there should be an international presence to guarantee the human rights of the Kosovar Serb minority. On the other hand, the independence of Republika Srpska or its annexation by Serbia could make the return of Muslim and Croat refugees and displaced persons (who represented the majority of the population before the war) even more difficult.

Independence of South Ossetia and Abkhazia might be acceptable provided all the displaced persons could return and receive compensation, and provided an international presence (not Russia) could guarantee their human rights. And of course there are other possible permutations that could be acceptable, provided they were reached through agreement among all the relevant parties.

■

A frequent argument on behalf of hard power is energy security. The United States is no longer self-sufficient in oil. The Ukrainian "gas wars" of 2005/2006 and 2009 exposed the dependence of Europe on Russian oil and gas. For emerging economies such as China and India, energy and raw materials are crucial to sustain economic growth. The United States, Russia, and China all tend to adopt a strategic rather than a market approach to energy security. Military power is needed, so goes the argument, to secure access to energy, especially oil and gas. This argument is part of a broader idea that the United States has to retain "command of the commons"—air, sea, and space.[29]

This kind of thinking is deeply embedded in a twentieth-century conception of hard security. In the two world wars, petroleum was defined as a "vital interest" because the military effort relied on motor vehicles, tanks, aircraft, and naval ships, all powered by oil. Both Germany and Japan depended on imported oil, and it is often argued that access to petroleum guided their strategic actions. This kind of thinking persisted during the Cold War years, when strategic reserves were built up on both sides, and remains important in scenario building and strategic planning in both the United States and Russia. Michael Klare, a specialist on resource conflicts, maintains that increasing competition between Russia, China, and the United States for energy supplies in the Persian Gulf, the Caspian, and Central Asia has led to a militarization of these areas.[30] According to Klare, the protection of U.S. oil and gas extraction is one of the reasons the United States created a military command structure for Africa (AFRICOM).[31]

What might be called the geopolitical approach to energy, however, no longer works in the context of twenty-first-century risks. In Iraq, despite the efforts to protect oil installations in the initial invasion, oil became a hugely important factor in the subsequent violence—oil was a factor in the sectarian conflict that raged through 2008, and oil rents, extracted through smuggling, looting, blowing up pipelines, or hostage taking, financed the violence. In the Caucasus, where Russia and the United States compete for influence, supposedly to gain access to oil, the competition for oil rents exacerbates instability and finances festering conflicts. The conflict in Chechnya, for example, was sustained for a long time through a mutual business between Chechen warlords and Russian generals; the former sold oil extracted from backyard oil wells to the latter, who, in turn, sold the oil received from the ministry of defense on the Moscow market.

Oil producers do, of course, use their dominance in energy supply as a political instrument. In 1973, Arab oil producers imposed an oil embargo on the West after the Yom Kippur War. Russia continues to subsidize oil and gas prices to former Soviet republics but in the event of political disagreements sometimes raises the price to commercial levels. Thus, it has cut off supplies or raised prices not only in the most publicized case of Ukraine but also in relation to Georgia, Lithuania, Estonia, and Belarus. Russia is not the only "offender" in this regard. Hugo Chávez often tries to use Venezuela's oil resources to reward or punish allies in Latin America. But does military power prevent this type of behavior? Or does it, like Ukraine's potential membership in NATO, provide a justification?

Geopolitics is based on the assumption that what matters is great power influence over states who deliver oil. This, however, is rarely the case. On the contrary, the competition for oil rents filters down through society. The biggest problem of contemporary oil producers has to do with governance. The days are over when oil installations could be insulated from popular pressure. At best, oil states like Saudi Arabia, Iran, Venezuela, and Azerbaijan survive on a mixture of patronage and repression, and are vulnerable to oil-price volatility. At worst, as in Iraq, they degenerate into weak states prone to violent upheavals. As two scholars at the Wilson Center put it: "[T]he United States, Europe, and Asia have not confronted the connection between foreign policies that tolerate or enable repression and corruption in many oil-producing countries, and the threats of terrorism, instability, and volatility they face today."[32]

The best way to achieve energy security is, first, through energy diversification, second through transparency of oil revenues, and third through human security. Energy diversification means investment in energy savings and alternative sources of energy. Transparency of oil revenues and pipeline payments helps to reduce endemic corruption. A human-security approach, as elaborated in this book, is the way to deal with the new risks that are exacerbated by competition for oil rents. And this applies to the broader argument about the global commons. After all, the main threat to trade routes today is piracy, not competing great powers.

Finally, energy security itself should be considered within a global rather than a national or a Western context. It should also include access to energy for every human being, including the poorest people. The focus on the security of energy supplies of industrialized countries and the competition among large energy importers risks ignoring the problem of energy poverty—the lack of access to heat or electricity or fuel in developing countries. In developing countries, high energy prices, or the disruption of fuel supply (oil-rich Nigeria regularly suffers from shortages of fuel), have much more grave consequences than those faced by developed consumer countries.

Energy security is a global problem linked to climate change and so, instead of geopolitical competition, there needs to be a global strategy that combines diversification, transparency, and human security.

■

An enduring example of geo-state politics, resistant to the notion of shared sovereignty, and wholly inimical to the concept of human rights, is the persistence of nuclear weaponry. Even the language of nuclear disarmament, as expressed by presidents Obama and Medvedev, and many other politicians around the world, confirms a twentieth-century view of sovereignty utterly at variance with the changing perspectives in a global era. It a bizarre anachronism that we have negotiated bans on land mines and cluster munitions on the grounds that these types of weapons inherently violate human rights and international humanitarian law on account of their indiscriminate nature, yet we treat nuclear weapons as though they might not.

The main argument for continuing to possess nuclear weapons is deterrence. That, after all, was the basis of the case for accumulating large numbers of nuclear weapons during the Cold War; they were supposed to deter an attack, whether conventional or unconventional, by the Soviet Union against the democracies of the West. But did they? It is often argued that deterrence kept the peace during the Cold War. Quite apart from the fact that there were many wars during this period outside of Western Europe and North America, the problem with this argument is that it can only be disproved, not proved. Had the Soviet Union attacked the West, then we would know that deterrence does not work. But we do not know whether the Soviet Union would have attacked the West had the West not possessed nuclear weapons. What we do know is that the arms race kept alive the idea of war — it was not peace but "imaginary war" that was experienced in Europe during the Cold War. Indeed, the arcane arguments about strategic, sub-strategic, and tactical weapons were all about how nuclear weapons might be used in the scenarios dreamed up by military planners. The term *arms control* has to be understood in the context of deterrence. It was about keeping alive the idea of war while minimizing the risks of such a war becoming real. Hence, arms control was directed against so-called defensive weapons and against sub-strategic or tactical weapons that were thought to be "usable," while preserving the capacity for "mutually assured destruction."

Since the end of the Cold War, we have plenty of proof that deterrence does not work. The American possession of nuclear weapons did not deter the 9/11 bombers—they inflicted mass destruction even if they did not use what are formally defined as weapons of mass destruction (WMDs)—nuclear, radiological, chemical, and biological weapons. Likewise, British nuclear weapons did not deter the use of polonium, which could be described as a radiological weapon (i.e., a WMD) according to the formal definition, to poison the Russian dissident Alexander Litvinov repeatedly in a Sushi Bar. A cartoon in the British magazine *Private Eye* showed Prime Minister Blair saying to Putin, "We need new nuclear weapons," and Putin replying, "Try Sushi."

Actually, President George W. Bush used a similar argument. In the National Security Strategy of 2002, it was argued that deterrence does not work against rogue states and terrorists. Suicide bombers and mad leaders do not fear retaliation; indeed, they might welcome retaliation since they do not care about human life and it would prove that they are involved in a war against the West. This explains Bush's emphasis on counter-force to deal with proliferation—hence the threats against Iran. But if leaders like Ahmadinejad are not rational, even a threat could be dangerous. And if deterrence only works against states that are rational, why do we need nuclear weapons at all? Surely no rational state would threaten to use them. We need another approach.

Nuclear weapons need to be reframed as a humanitarian issue, and deterrence needs to be reframed as prevention. In particular, nuclear weapons should be criminalized. The threat or use of nuclear weapons should be treated as a war crime or a crime against humanity and should be included in the jurisdiction of the International Criminal Court. Since a nuclear war could destroy the world, everything must be done to prevent a nuclear war from happening—not through threats, which risk provoking mad reactions, but through the type of strategies discussed in this book

It is often said that nuclear weapons cannot be disinvented. That is true, but the knowledge of how to make nuclear weapons does not reside in a single individual but in social infrastructure that involves a complex combination of specific skills, knowledge, and equipment. States alone have the capacity to build such infrastructures. The current fear is that terrorists will get hold of nuclear materials. But terrorists could not construct their own infrastructure. They would need access to states. Thus, the best way to prevent this from happening is to dismantle the global nuclear infrastructure, and this would require extensive international monitoring and verification that would further strengthen the interconnection of states. Perhaps the most important task is to break the link between nuclear weapons and great-power status, something that would involve a profound change in global public discourse—a shift from geopolitics to human security.

Absolute state sovereignty, war mentality, territorial inviolability, and aspects of superpower rivalry are remnants of the industrial and imperial age. But hard power is hard to shift. The twentieth-century wars established huge embedded institutions in our societies, both in the West and among the newly emerging great powers like Russia, China, and India. Dictators oppose interference. The left fears imperialism. Organizations don't like change. Statesmen, soldiers, and civil servants naturally think the way they have always done things is the right way to do things. Moreover, the identity of the state is often bound up with a militarized notion of security. Thus, the War on Terror was a popular policy because it reflected popular assumptions about the nature of American power, however out of date. In the same way, it is helpful for Iran, China, and Russia to have a Western enemy. But these are old battles and old wars, and there's no virtue in fighting them again. Traditional military power no longer works as a way of dealing with potential spoilers like Russia, China, Iran, and North Korea; indeed, perceiving them as military threats may have the opposite effect of what is intended—legitimizing the buildup of armaments as well as domestic repression. Instead, such states need to be embedded in an interconnected global framework aimed at protecting the human security of all citizens. Traditional ways of thinking about security need to be reformulated. Sovereignty is no longer absolute; today, states are members of an international system that operates on behalf of the human community and in which all human lives are considered equal. Energy security is a global, not a national, problem. Deterrence, which is an unprovable strategy until it fails, needs to be recast as prevention since a nuclear war is the worst imaginable cataclysm.

Above all, war itself needs to be reframed as a human catastrophe, along with natural disasters, famines, and pandemics. Human security is about prevention and avoidance of human catastrophes, rather than protecting us against their aftereffects.

8

Africa: A Beacon of Hope?

Human security will find its greatest test, and perhaps make its greatest accomplishments, in Africa. In part, that's because Africans are the originators of the concept. They understand security in a very particular, very immediate way. As one ambassador put it to Beebe,

> You Americans are always looking for terrorists and weapons of mass destruction. Yes, we do have those things in Africa. We have terrorism. Our terrorism is poverty, HIV/AIDS, and malaria. We have weapons of mass destruction as well. It is an AK-47, usually carried by a child. All of this is played out every day in an environment we don't even control.

It was an oppressively hot Sunday in September 2009 when Beebe found himself part of a delegation being escorted through the town of Huambo, Angola, from the regional military headquarters to the newly renovated military hospital. Beyond the gates of the hospital, a curious line of hospital staff were waiting for the visitors. The purpose of the trip was rather innocuous: to discover the role and effectiveness of the hospital in providing treatment for HIV in the military. After all, this was a military hospital.

The chief doctor, a captain in the Angolan army, briefed the delegation on the state of the hospital just a few years earlier: the building was near collapse, the interior of the hospital was completely dilapidated, and there were no sterile areas for surgery. Pictures showed patients lying on cots, on the floor, and outside. There was precious little equipment; what there was didn't work. Most of the patients in the hospital appeared to be civilians. As the doctor proudly continued his presentation about how the hospital had been revitalized and now had beds for patients, a pharmacy, and a surgical ward, one member of the delegation raised what seemed to be the obvious question: "You service *only* the military and their dependents here, correct?" The young doctor, a bit puzzled, looked up and said, "Why no. Over 60 percent of the people we see here have nothing to do with the military." The delegate was baffled "Well, why don't they just go to the local hospital? Is the service here *that* much better?" The young doctor smiled gently and said, "No, sir. We are the only hospital in the entire region. This is the only place anyone can go for medicine. Many of the patients we see are carried by their families over fifty kilometers. How can we turn them away, sir?"

The doctor's statement was not surprising. Militaries' roles and perceptions of security in Africa have always been quite different from those in the United States and other Western countries. We simply don't understand what constitutes security in the minds of Africans. Yet, until the West stops trying to impose what *we* feel is right for African security and begins listening to what *Africans* say is relevant, we will never be able to contribute in a positive way to this hugely important continent.

As the senior Africa analyst on the U.S. Army staff, Beebe had the job of discovering how Africans defined security. After researching the question in fifteen different countries, he found that the base philosophy of what constitutes a threat for the United States—and other Western countries—is quite different from the way Africans conceive of threats to themselves. While Western language defines security through a lens of military threat—planes, tanks, defense budgets, and standing armies along a border prepared to go on the offensive—African security—or insecurity—is best defined as *conditions*-based. Most Africans talked about security in terms of security-sector reform, health, poverty, and environmental shock caused by climate change. The tremendous droughts and food shortages of 2008 suggested that food security might be at the very top of security concerns in Africa.

Of course, security is debated in Africa like everywhere else. There are still political and military elites who stick to traditional state–centered views. And for many Africans, human security is a way of critiquing these views. Do states actually protect and ensure the welfare of their people; how can they do better; how can they be made accountable when they fail?

The African perspective of human security changes how the world looks—from top to bottom. The conventional global map divides continental land masses into the sovereign states that have made up what we have known as the international system since the end of World War II. This image of the world, in which the territorial state is the overriding definition of authority and security, was a "system" that was constructed—by both East and West—and imposed on the developing world during the nineteenth and twentieth centuries.

In this Western-biased state-sovereign system, the state reigned supreme and was the focal object of international discourse and military protection/defense. Conventional militaries were identified with national security; their job was to protect the state from enemies. At the same time, they constituted a potential threat to opposing states. In the twentieth century, the state maintained relative hegemony over what have been called elements of national power:

diplomatic tools, control of information and its dissemination, military power projection, and economic viability. State sovereignty was paramount, although additional legal frameworks were constructed to adjudicate international infractions. Indeed, the United States championed the development of most of these international agencies, organizations, and bodies after the end of World War II.

Security alliances were an essential element in this structure. NATO, for example, was formed as an organization to represent a group of states, with Article 5 explicitly stating that an attack on one ally would be considered an attack on all. Elsewhere, states were divided up according to positions in the Cold War—they were pro-West, pro-Soviet, or nonaligned. These positions mattered much more than what was going on inside states. Many leaders in what was known as the third world—the Idi Amins and Mobutu Sese Sekos—were known to be ruthless, oppressive, and dictatorial, but because the world was divided into two poles, intervention in these countries was only carried out when it was in the self-interest of one—or both—of those poles. Seldom were actions carried out based on the needs of people. Nowhere was this more obvious than on the African continent, where the United States and the Soviet Union played a brutal game of tit for tat using African states as pieces. Populations in these oppressive and oppressed states had little voice in their own affairs and little way of telling the rest of the world the conditions they had to put up with.

During the twentieth century, a discussion of security would have been incomplete without a brief mention of protecting the economic viability of the state. Economic power was guaranteed by state military prowess, or so it was assumed, until multinational corporations blurred the line that separated national from international interest. Economic ties were formed with allies with an understanding that each state had a vested interest in protecting those economic links. A multitrillion-dollar military-industrial complex was developed to support and defend this system. It worked well as long as the world was bipolar and the other guys were doing the same thing. In short, we all played with the same rule book, bending and breaking the rules where we could.

This was the way we viewed the world—through the prism of state-based enemies and threats similar to ourselves. Yet, what happened to the United States—and the world—on September 11, 2001, was an attack not launched from inside the system, not instigated by a state, and certainly not symmetric. There will be volumes written on the "failures of intelligence" to identify this new type of threat, yet in the final analysis, it has to be understood in terms of the way conditions of insecurity allow new actors to leverage twenty-first-century technologies and create subterranean international networks.

The second-most-crippling attack on the United States was launched just a few short years later, in August 2005. Again, this attack was not launched from inside the system, not instigated by a state following the rules of sovereign interaction, and certainly not symmetric. This attack was not masterminded by one group bent on the destruction of the United States, but the second- and third-order effects of it rippled throughout the entire country. The attacker this time was Hurricane Katrina.

Conditions-based threats, or "creeping vulnerabilities," such as natural calamities or networks of extremists are commonplace on the African continent. So what would the world of security look like if we adopted a conditions-based, African approach?

Worldmapper.org, is a collaborative effort between the University of Michigan and the University of Sheffield to create cartograms that show what the world "really looks like." It is one way of representing the world through African eyes. Cartograms are simply graphical representations of data. The cartograms "grow" or "shrink" countries according to the prevalence or absence of the criterion. In global cartograms of HIV/AIDS and malaria deaths, Africa appears as a bloated mass, by far the dominant shape. North America and Europe practically vanish, as do even China and India in the malaria map, though India remains a significant mass on the HIV/AIDS map.

When the criterion is switched to poverty, Africa is a substantial bloc matched or exceeded by parts of the Middle East, China, and the Indian subcontinent. However, when deaths as a result of drought is the criterion, Africa is without equal anywhere in the world. Almost every other country is eliminated from the cartogram because deaths from lack of potable water have been eliminated from the world—except Africa, where they occur on a massive scale.

Finally, when the criterion is child labor, the cartograms show that the phenomenon is quite well distributed, though it is almost invisible in Europe and North America. But the size of the problem in Africa is self-evident. What these "catastrophe" cartograms make clear is that threats related to the basic needs of daily life—safe food, drinking water, medicine, and opportunities for education and self-improvement (things that are denied to any child in the labor force)—are vast and utterly predominant in Africa. These massive challenges—rendered as such in the distortions of the cartograms—are at the heart of human insecurity from Cape Town to Cairo, Dakar to Mogadishu.

Challenges such as these would test to the breaking point governments' legitimacy and capacity to respond in the developed world. The challenges facing African states expose the powerlessness of states—at worst, an absence of political will, and at best, an inability to deliver. The security architecture is no more than a house of cards. None of these conditions (HIV/AIDS, poverty, famine, and child labor) alone presents an overwhelming security "threat," yet when even one of those cards is pulled, it is enough to collapse the entire house. Additionally, the impact of these conditions-based security concerns doesn't stop at the border — it extends to groups of people whose cultural and tribal lineages spread over multiple borders.

The geopolitical borders of most African states were, of course, determined not by Africans but by the Berlin Conference of 1884–1885. Many African national borders make sense from a Western perspective but have little relevance to ethnic or tribal cultures divided between several countries, little impact on herdsmen traveling with their herds in search of fertile grazing lands and water, and little real significance for indigenous populations who cross these borders as part of their everyday lives. What this means is that the governments in power are not necessarily representative of the populations but of interest groups and subgroups within the states.

If the West continues to demand adherence to a traditional view of security, we risk becoming marginalized in the eyes of those who most need a sustainable definition for security. If you went to the doctor with a sore throat, only to have the doctor place you on the examination table, break one leg, then declare the problem not to be a sore throat but a broken leg, how often would you go back for treatment? To retain any relevance in the eyes of Africans, the West will have to shift from imposing what we see as the right definition of security on Africa to supporting what Africans see as a relevant definition for their own security. During a discussion at the Pentagon, in 2007 a senior African military attaché pointed out, "Most people in my country don't like the military and don't want the military in their cities." Beebe anticipated the reasons: the militaries are predatory, dangerous, supportive of the regime, and corrupt. But as the African attaché continued, it was clear that his reason was far more practical:

> Our people don't like us because they do not see us as value added to society or to the development of our countries. You, the United States, want to train us on peacekeeping but don't want to give us training on how to be doctors, or how to build roads

and bridges. Teach us about water and sanitation and how to help our countries develop. This is what will keep the peace, you see.

For Africa to be successful in the twenty-first century, it will need to become less militaristic. The 2007 Human Security Report Project indicates that conflicts in sub-Saharan Africa are steadily decreasing in both number and lethality. In 2002, there were thirteen state-based conflicts. By 2006, the number had dropped to seven. Yet, this does not mean Africa is becoming any more stable. One of the main reasons for the decline in conflicts has been the way in which the United Nations has brokered cease-fires and deployed peacekeepers to maintain those cease-fires. Since 1999, the number of personnel deployed in multilateral peace missions in Africa has been increasing at a staggering rate—from 4,853 civilian and military personnel deployed in seven missions in 1999 to 76,814 personnel deployed across sixteen missions in 2009. The challenge is how to bring about a sustainable peace without the need for international peacekeepers.

What is needed in Africa is a blending of police, military, and development experts to create an organization along the lines of a civilian protection and development corps. Nowhere in the world is the concept of engagement brigades more applicable than in Africa. While the West continues to impose a bifurcated, Western model of military and police upon Africa, it has also created a dangerous competition over scarce resources among the different powerful and potentially *destabilizing* security organizations, especially between militaries and police. While one organization will often receive the lion's share of resources through foreign military training, the organization that lacks resources may take to looting, stealing, or worse from the populations it is supposed to protect. In North Kivu, a province in eastern Democratic Republic of the Congo (DRC), when Beebe visited in 2008, police officers were earning an average of about $7 per month, mainly because each corrupt level of government was taking a cut. Even by African standards, this was nowhere near enough to survive. So, the police resorted to setting up roadblocks and patrolling for bribes. Most frustrating was the thought that had the very simple concepts of mobile banking been used, police would have been ensured adequate pay and would not have resorted to being part of the security challenge.

A better way would be to take the senior African military attaché's advice and facilitate the transformation of military and police units into engagement brigades that add value to their countries. This would mean doing away with trying to create forces in the Western image. Of course, the engagement brigades must be able to provide security in dangerous situations and be able to contribute to African peacekeeping. That means they have to be able to perform human-security operations rather than traditional war fighting. They need to be taught not to fight military enemies but to protect people, to create humanitarian space and, in the process, to fight the conditions of instability. They need to be taught how to operate in support of law and order under rules of engagement more akin to those of police forces than those of militaries.

Because engagement brigades are not the same as militaries, they can undertake civilian tasks as well. Units could be designated to provide heavy engineering support for development of roads, bridges, and other types of infrastructure. The vocational training developed in such engagement brigades could then be used in the civilian sector once brigade personnel were released from service. Africa suffers immensely from two factors in this respect—large standing military forces with little to do and a civilian sector grossly deficient in skilled labor. The creation of engagement brigades would remedy both problems. When Beebe visited the chief of Angolan Defense Forces (CHOD), the general was asked why the Angolan military had not reduced its forces as it had promised. The general answered directly:

We have approximately 155,000 personnel. We would like to have only 120,000. However, do you expect us to put 35,000 people on the street when the only skills they have are basic military skills? How does that help the stability and development of our country? We want our military to be a vehicle for the development of our country, not its detriment.

Africa also suffers from a lack of adequate housing. Engagement brigades could be developed to tackle this shortage too. Angola is pioneering a potential solution by converting traditional mechanized infantry units into rapid engineering and construction units with the assistance of a remarkable machine that very few people in the West have heard of. Yet in Africa it could prove to be a more powerful "weapon" than an M1 tank or F-16 fighter. According to its manufacturer, MIC Industries, the Ultimate Building Machine (UBM) is a self-contained factory on wheels capable of fabricating and assembling an entire building at remote construction sites. Traditional construction time is shortened, since UBM-made steel buildings require no screws, bolts, fasteners, beams, trusses, or columns. The machine is programmed at the site or remotely, and then fed a roll of steel that it bends into panels to create a permanent shelter. A crew of ten to twelve trained skilled workers can assemble a building as large as 10,000 square feet in a single day. The training to master the equipment takes less than two days.

Technical fixes alone are not the answer. The engagement brigades would be asked to consult with the local population about what kind of houses are most appropriate and how best to build them quickly and efficiently.

Rapid-construction engagement brigades could provide housing for thousands within a matter of weeks. Other engagement brigades could work on power supply, prioritizing lightweight, long- duration renewable energy—solar and wind power—water supply, and sanitation. In this way, militaries and police forces can transform themselves from twentieth-century operations competing for scarce resources and preying on their own populations to twenty-first-century vehicles for social development and bedrocks of skilled labor forces. The West should support a shift in training and manning philosophies away from creating defense forces aimed at armed threats to a security-engagement-brigade model oriented around combating the conditions of instability and hindrances to development.

Assisting in the conversion of defense forces will be challenging for Western militaries that don't have a lot of "development" skills and expertise themselves. We will have to look outside the traditional military lanes of training. One such effort, the STAR-TIDES project, is a consortium run out of the National Defense University in Washington, D.C. Beebe first met the director of STAR-TIDES, Dr. Linton Wells, in 2007. STAR (Sustainable Technologies, Accelerated Research) TIDES (is a research effort to encourage information sharing and develop communities of interest to support populations under stress). STAR-TIDES promotes affordable, sustainable support. It has operated and conducted research in most parts of the globe with a solid record of success. STAR-TIDES has also been successful in breaking down barriers and building bridges between business, civil society, and government stakeholders working toward a common goal. This organization is well suited to help the transformation of African engagement brigades. Where a human-security framework conceptualizes the nexus of defense and development, STAR-TIDES has put it into practice.

How necessary for security is this? According to the 2009 UN Millennium Development Goals Report, more than 62 percent of sub-Saharan African populations live without access to water and sanitation, durable housing, or adequate living space. Africa also lives in the dark, literally, with more than 74 percent of the total population having no access to electricity. The numbers are even more staggering for rural populations, which also tend to be most vulnerable during times of near conflict and conflict. Africa is the only continent where, according to International Energy Agency estimates, there will be more people living without electricity in 2030 than there are now.

Health Care

The lack of adequate health care and health facilities are crippling the development and security of Africa. Child mortality rates are the highest of any continent: one child in every six will not reach his or her fifth birthday. This drives women to have more children, which removes them from the productive workplace and limits their opportunities. In 2006, roughly 1 million people worldwide died of malaria; 95 percent were Africans. Neglected tropical diseases (NTDs), most of which are parasitic diseases spread by worms, flies, mosquitoes, and snails, are widespread among the rural-poor populations of sub-Saharan Africa. These diseases cause disabilities, impaired growth, and disfigurement. Additionally, they destroy the agricultural workforce that could be producing food for the continent. Delivering rapid-impact medications for the seven most prevalent diseases (ascariasis, trichuriasis, hookworm infection, schistosomiasis, lymphatic filariasis, trachoma, and onchocerciasis) would cost as little as $0.40 to $0.79 *per person per year*. It is estimated that a five-year program to control or eliminate the major neglected tropical diseases in sub-Saharan Africa could cost approximately $1 billion to $2 billion, or approximately $7 to $9 per year for each individual in Africa.

Health facilities are few and far between in most parts of Africa. The possibility of transforming militaries from defense forces to security forces capable of guaranteeing safe spaces in which they can also contribute to safeguarding, building, and stocking hospi-

tals is not unrealistic. Traditionally, many NGOs and private volunteer organizations have been resistant to working with militaries. The thought of working to support a *military* hospital is
anathema to many within the NGO community, until—as in
Huambo, Angola—they see that the majority of the patients are
civilians. If militaries were transformed into engagement brigades,
this skepticism would melt away.

Health security is one area where various communities of interest can effectively fuse resources to make a meaningful and sustainable impact. Too many times conference attendees lament, "We
are not doing enough in Africa. We need to do more." The regret
should be that we aren't doing *enough together* in Africa. That's how
Dr. John Howe, president of Project HOPE, sees it. Project HOPE
is one of the oldest and most respected health NGOs in the United
States. Dr. Howe's organization has been groundbreaking in its will-
ingness to work with militaries on health issues in Africa. Much of
their work has been assisting in the development of projects for the
Africa Partnership Station (APS), an effort by the U.S. Navy to reach
out to African nations through educational programs, health programs, environmental-security training, and small-scale building
programs. When the effort began, many NGOs were hesitant to
take up the offer by the U.S. military to ride on Navy ships. Project
HOPE understood the value of being able to combine efforts and
resources. Now that APS has made several voyages and the results
are being felt, others are opening up to the idea. Project HOPE continues to help direct this effort in the health arena to ensure sustainable engagement.

Poverty

Africa is the wealthiest continent below the ground and the poorest
above the ground. In terms of development indicators, sub-Saharan

Africa is lagging behind other developing regions. Fifty-one percent of the population in sub-Saharan Africa lives in extreme poverty (i.e., less than $1.25 a day), compared to 25 percent in other developing regions. Since 1990, only little progress has been made—in 1990, 57 percent of sub-Saharan Africans were living in extreme poverty. The ramifications of the recent global economic crisis have yet to be accounted for, and some estimate that this will push the number living in extreme poverty back to 1990 levels.

While the West continues to invest millions of dollars in aid for poverty reduction, a trip to one of the poorest areas in Kinshasa, Democratic Republic of the Congo, shows what $10 can do. Nathan Hulley, the managing director of a microfinance fund called Hope International, took Beebe to a small convenience store. He explained that a lady known simply as "Mamma" had taken a $5 loan to bake bread. Mamma paid the loan back within the month and took a $10 loan, which she repaid the next month. She continued to take loans and pay them back until she could afford to stock a room with goods. She opened her own convenience store. "It's sort of a 7-Eleven, Congo style," Hulley joked. When Beebe asked where Mamma started out, Hulley took him about twenty meters to a milk carton halfway down a filthy alley. "This is where we first met Mamma, and I'm pretty sure that's the same milk carton." Microfinance projects have helped improve the lives of Congolese in the most impoverished areas of Kinshasa. Many now have the money to pay for their children's school. Many have bought their first books and are teaching each other to read English. Others simply use one loan to work their way along to afford the next. Amazingly, Hulley said,

> We haven't had a single person default on a loan. I think we're up to around 1,000 loans at this point. There's really not a catch. We give loans to groups of people—up to twenty people within

the group. During the time of the loan, we also talk with them about managing their money, managing inventory, business stuff. They also know that they're responsible for each other's success. If one person in the group doesn't pay back the loan, then the group is responsible for paying the loan back or everyone in the group is excluded from receiving another loan. We haven't had a problem with any of that, though. They've actually created a business cooperative and are discussing creating their own loans now. It's pretty much turned this area into one of the best market centers in Kinshasa. They've taken ownership of their future.

One of the great attempts of Western governments toward Africa has been the attempt to artificially stimulate the creation of civil society, good governance, and democracy. Yet, none of these are created in a vacuum, and Africans haven't bought in to the idea that the West holds the patent on all of those things. What we see when we give people the dignity of work and the ability to take ownership of their own future is quite remarkable and defies the greatest attempts of big government. People aren't destined to be impoverished their entire lives if given the tools to build better futures for themselves. Contrary to popular Western beliefs, Africans are quite resourceful and entrepreneurial when given the slightest opportunity. Five dollars in Mamma's hands makes far more impact than $5 million in the coffers of a corrupt or inefficient ministry.

Impact of Climate Change

Climate change will be one of the most urgent security concerns for Africa in the twenty-first century. The coastal population of Africa is expected to increase nearly 80 percent over the next decade from an estimated 141 million to nearly 256 million. Any rise in sea level, or the arrival of hurricanes on the continent, within the next two decades could cripple parts of Africa and place tremendous stress on the international community. An event on the scale of Hurricane Katrina in Port Harcourt or Lagos, Nigeria, or Cabinda, Angola, would not only be an international humanitarian crisis but also would bring world energy markets to their knees. Climate change is real and is already making significant impacts on the African continent. The march of the Sahara Desert southward has forced herdsmen from their traditional grazing lands.

As with all creeping vulnerabilities, we will never be able to say definitively, but many argue that the conflict in Darfur is the first climate-change conflict. The tragedy in Darfur certainly provides an example of the kind of conflict that might result from environmental stress. And this is just one of many. The International Federation of Red Cross and Red Crescent Societies estimated that 2001 was the first year that environmental refugees outnumbered war refugees in Africa. The impacts of climate change are being felt more and more in all parts of the continent. In the north, populations are being forced farther south each year, which is creating pressures on already-stretched natural resources. As water becomes scarcer in these areas, the stresses build. Egypt has openly stated that any attempt to dam the waters from the Nile would be grounds for war.

While the effects of climate change continue to create more potential flash points on the African continent, the West still debates whether climate change exists. What we have to realize is this: perception is reality on the African continent. There, as an African ambassador told Beebe, the perception is that the West is to blame for climate change yet has done very little to mitigate the impacts of climate change on Africans. This potential threat could be turned into an opportunity for greater engagement with Africa. On a continent that has some of the rarest flora and fauna in the world, the global community has a responsibility to protect that which has no voice—our natural environment.

There is a great deal for all sides to gain by working together to mitigate both climate change and environmental shock. Environmental shock takes into account natural and man-made disasters such as remnants of war (e.g., unexploded ordnance and land mines.) Of greatest promise is the potential collaboration of engagement brigades with conservation and environmental groups such as the World Conservation Society, World Wildlife Fund, the Nature Conservancy, Water Advocates, the International Union for Conservation of Nature, and even Greenpeace. Environmental shock takes many forms on the African continent. It is difficult to say which is most pressing. Among the most discussed are the illegal timbering operations happening across the continent and illegal fishing off the coasts, which is made possible by the lack of military/security capacity to patrol national waters. There are solid connections between instability and environmental destruction.

■

Lao Tzu is credited with saying, "Give a man a fish to feed him for a day; teach a man to fish and feed him for a lifetime." In thinking about human security in Africa, the phrase might be turned into a question: what happens when a man is already a fisherman and you take all his fish away? In the Somali case the answer would be, you create a pirate. The weakness of Siad Barre's Somali state in the 1990s, coupled with the lucrative fishing waters of the Gulf of Aden, led to overfishing by European and East Asian fleets, which devastated fish stocks. Somalis stood by helplessly and watched their livelihoods being hauled away from them. With the decline of the traditional Somali fishing industry paired with the ever-declining control of the central government, piracy became not only lucrative as a criminal enterprise but also a last resort of starving Somali fishermen. Piracy is illegal, reprehensible, and cannot be excused, but people living in desperation make desperate decisions.

Western governments are now more engaged in patrolling the Gulf of Aden to protect the sea lanes and identify the threat of piracy in kinetic terms. Pirates—especially those who threaten vessels bearing Western flags or oil tankers—are killed or captured, and Western nations are quick to search for links between pirates and larger terrorist schemes. Meanwhile, young Somali men continue to brave waters hundreds of miles off the Somali coast in vessels that are barely seaworthy in hopes of capturing a ship to bring their criminal handlers millions of dollars and their families a few more days of survival. What the West has yet to understand is that when one has nothing left to live for, one is prepared to die for almost anything. That is a basic algorithm of human (in)security.

The challenges facing Africa are so many and so diverse that the luxury of parceling them out between organizations, or hoping that Western NGOs can turn up in time to remedy a disaster after the event, does not exist. African security, meaning the lives of African men, women, and children, cannot be treated so casually or sporadically. Nor, on a continent where the infrastructure is often basic and one of the few existent institutional blocks that is recognized as having some authority is the military, is it possible to manage human security in Africa without the help of Western and African militaries. Armies must change in order to be effective; but they cannot afford to be ignored. Time and again, militaries possess the tools for the solution, but NGOs, governments, and academics hesitate to engage with military organizations.

Beebe was lamenting this conundrum to co-workers in the Pentagon cafeteria when a short, stocky man walked up to him. "I heard you say you needed to get a bunch of people together from a lot of different places to learn from each other," he said. "I can do that for you." Beebe looked at the man who stood focusing squarely and very intently back at him. Beebe asked, "How would you propose to do that? Do you organize conferences? I don't have a budget and I'm not so sure how hip most NGOs and academics would be to coming into the Pentagon. It would cost an arm and a leg to get people here." Still focused intently on Beebe, the man said, "I do organize conferences, among other things. But it won't cost you an arm and a leg. As a matter of fact, it won't cost you anything. I'm a builder in virtual reality. I'll help you create your own world, and people from anywhere can come there to research, meet, discuss ideas, and get to know each other. I've spent over a year's worth of time in virtual reality. I'm Jaque Davison."

Beebe and Davison together began to create the Africa InfoSphere for people working in Africa. The Africa InfoSphere is a virtual world built using a platform launched from a Web site created by the company ActiveWorlds. A visitor to the Africa InfoSphere can access various one-dimensional Web sites dealing with Africa and a selection of "pavilions" featuring topics that are of primary interest to Africans: the economy, eco treasures, agriculture, disease, water, and conflict. A pavilion is a virtual room where websites, links, webcams, and live feeds can be placed dealing with a specific topic. Davison is fond of using the example of the Conflict Pavilion and how it would take the average web surfer over 7 days to discover all of the links and information that is at the fingertips of Africa InfoSphere users immediately upon entry. Each pavilion contains a virtual conference room, as Davison had promised. In total, Davison estimates it would take an average person seventy days of surfing the Internet twelve hours a day to find the weblinks and other relevant information that is readily available within the Africa InfoSphere. In addition to enabling meaningful research in reduced time, the Africa InfoSphere can connect visitors to others working on similar or complementary projects anywhere in the world. International barriers and information silos begin to crumble. In times of natural disaster or humanitarian crisis in Africa, it has traditionally taken the international community days or weeks to establish a crisis-reaction center simply because it takes so long for crisis-response workers to travel to the region. Using the Africa InfoSphere, a crisis-reaction center responsible for international communications and coordination of logistics could be set up in a matter of hours. Additionally, since there would be no travel involved, more people could be deployed to work on the challenge. People wouldn't have to leave their normal work spaces; they wouldn't be separated from their networks of experts; and they would have continuous access to computer and phone systems. Information could be forwarded from the crisis-reaction center to aid workers and security forces at the point of impact through the Africa InfoSphere, since it works on cell phones. The Africa InfoSphere can also be accessed by a computer in the field running a connection as slow as 56k. All of this would increase the international community's capacity to efficiently respond to the crisis at hand. And the cost to build the Africa Infosphere? About twenty hours from Jaque Davison and three pots of coffee for Beebe.

Since the development of the Africa InfoSphere, hundreds of Africanists, NGOs, academics, and others have been able to make connections from all over the world. The value of these connections may never be known, but, as Jaque Davison says, the goal is to eliminate the six degrees of separation between where one sits and the knowledge one needs.

Security on the African continent in the twenty-first century will be less about kinetic threats and more about the conditions creating human insecurities and draining populations of hope. Individuals who commit criminal terrorist acts aren't born; they are created through years of deprivation, disenfranchisement, and desperation. Security of the twenty-first century will be less and less about sovereign state interactions and more about proactively identifying causes of instability. Africans are quick to point to the lingering evils of colonialism. Recently, with the advent of the U.S. military command for Africa, AFRICOM, and the increased activity of China on the continent, there has been renewed discussion of neo-colonialism, which Africans chafe against—and rightfully so. Yet, what is probably more accurate and less discussed is African *neo-medievalism*. Most decisions are made in each nation's capital city by a de facto "king's court." Neo-medievalism is reproduced in African society because of the way many Africans see themselves as servants of the state. Western governments have fallen into the trap of spending exorbitant amounts of time in capital cities with oligarchies while neglecting the provinces where many instabilities take root as a result of neglect. This is not a recipe for success. Our diplomatic communities, aid communities, and others must reverse this troubling trend if we are to have meaningful impacts on African societies.

Outsiders tend to be preoccupied with what they see as problems of governance—the corruption and dysfunction of a "king's court." But if they were to focus on what *can* be done at local levels in the provinces, then it might be possible to rebuild governance from the bottom up. Security is bound up with legitimacy. By providing security in a holistic sense, it is possible to establish the political space in which Africans can themselves agree on the sort of governance they need.

9

The Ultimate Weapon

The F-22 Raptor was conceived in the early 1980s as a radar-evading, advanced fighter jet to take on the Soviet air force. It was recast in the 1990s so that it would be able to hit ground targets as well. According to enthusiasts, the F-22

> is an amazing plane, which combines all the desired attributes of a fighter: stealth, speed, maneuverability, the ability to fly at great height and do so economically without using too much fuel. It is intended to control the skies through the coming decades and is the centerpiece of how the U.S. Air Force intends to operate in the future.[1]

Lockheed, its manufacturer, says that the F-22 "is designed primarily to be first sent into battle to take down air and ground defenses, helped by its advanced stealth capabilities that give it a radar signature roughly the size of a bumblebee."[2] For kinetic warfare, the F-22 is the ultimate weapon.

The F-22 is hugely expensive—the entire cost of 183 airplanes is nearly $70 billion.[3] Forty-four states in the United States are involved in its production, and continued production is often defended as a way of sustaining skilled manufacturing jobs. But the

F-22 was designed to match air power that no other state possesses or, even allowing for renewed armament by China and Russia, is likely to possess in the near future. The cost of this overmatch design made the F-22 much too expensive to be risked in conflicts. As Defense Secretary Gates himself pointed out in testimony to Congress: "The reality is that we are fighting two wars in Iraq and Afghanistan and the F-22 has not performed a single mission in either theater."[4]

The argument for weapons like the F-22 is conventional deterrence based on military threats. The F-22 is intended to deter a war with another great power—another sovereign state—presumably Russia or China, even though interstate war is on the decline. The only wars between states in the twenty-first century have been between India and Pakistan, Iraq and the United States, and Georgia and Russia. Indeed, wars involving states in general are on the decline. The Uppsala Conflict Data Program (UCDP) shows that the number of wars involving states and involving more than 1,000 deaths in battle has declined from twenty-one in 1999 to sixteen in 2008, of which the vast majority were civil wars.[5] This decline cannot be attributed to ultimate weapons designed for deterrence; the F-22 is not the reason there has been no war with Russia or China. Yet the decline of state-based wars does not mean greater stability or security for the world in which we live.

Non-state conflicts and what the UCDP calls one-sided violence against civilians are increasingly common, especially in sub-Saharan Africa. These are conflicts involving militias, criminal groups, warlords, mujahideen, mercenaries, and normal people, as well as remnants of state security forces. They are the "new wars" that we have tried to describe in this book. They typify the violent upheavals of the twenty-first century; they represent the culmination, as we have argued, of a set of "vulnerabilities"—conditions like poverty, disease, lawlessness, exclusive ideologies, and environmental degradation. And in these conflicts, the F-22 has no place.

Indeed, even the wars in Iraq and Afghanistan could be viewed as exceptions—anomalies caused by the military invasions of 2001 and 2003. It was the application of conventional military force in fragile situations that ignited the persistent conflicts we have witnessed in both countries. Quantitative analysis of contemporary conflicts has shown that these two wars are outliers in terms of both intensity and method of warfare.[6] There was no Al-Qaeda in Iraq before the U.S. invasion—Iraq became a theater attracting extreme Islamists from all over the world who saw Iraq as an opportunity to attack the United States and to foment chaos. Today, after the surge and after the sectarian fighting has died down, Al-Qaeda is the main problem in Iraq. In Afghanistan, where the coalition operations had much more global sympathy, conventional force did succeed initially in destroying the Al-Qaeda camps, but, in the aftermath of the fall of the Taliban, the focus has remained on chasing so-called terrorists to the detriment of broader Afghan security. The aerial attacks on terrorist strongholds and the collateral damage have, like in Iraq, attracted more recruits, while neglect of the needs of the Afghan population has provided opportunities that terrorists could exploit. The hated Taliban is returning in alliance with Al-Qaeda. We are creating more terrorists than we are killing.

Iraq and Afghanistan are not precedents for future conflicts, unless the United States or other military powers intend to invade other countries, and there seems little sign of that. The many insecure areas of the world are characterized by so-called weak states and a toxic mixture of criminal and political violence that sets the stage for the kind of vulnerabilities described in this book. The experience of Iraq and Afghanistan shows that the application of conventional military force in such situations can make things much worse. That does not mean we should do nothing. On the contrary, how to address this complicated mix of deadly ingredients that travels across the world is the challenge of twenty-first-century security. It is prevention, not deterrence, that matters.

We have looked for answers to this challenge from those who live insecurely on a daily basis—in Africa, the Balkans, Iraq, and Afghanistan. The evidence suggests that a human-security approach is needed in Iraq, Afghanistan, and Pakistan. Such an approach would include the population-security strategies adopted by General Petraeus and General McChrystal, but it needs to be civilian-led and even more attentive to local lives. Drone attacks, for example, would be unacceptable. The F-22 would not be useful at all. A human-security approach would emphasize bottom-up reconstruction of governance and justice systems, local security capabilities, and, of course, addressing poverty, education, and health. It would, as well, have to be part of a more global strategy for dealing with the transnational criminal networks, especially drug networks, that are nourished by and that nourish conflicts. The challenge in Iraq and Afghanistan is to see whether two conflicts begun as conventional military engagements can be transformed by the same actors that began them. This is no small task; it may be impossible.

But a set of proactive policies in regions that have not yet reached the levels of violence of Iraq and Afghanistan and where life is often intolerable is essential. Parts of the world face a crisis of insecurity, and globalization tells us that what starts in one place can have consequences everywhere. That is the world we live in. There is a huge mismatch in our current response to insecurity. We spend billions of dollars on the F-22 and other "ultimate weapons systems" that are completely unusable in *all* contemporary zones of insecurity.

The neo-medievalism referred to in Chapter 8 is not limited to Africa. As happened in the early modern period, in many parts of the world, states have lost their monopoly on violence. Protection gangs, private security companies, and local strongmen are called in because of the absence of public security. If we fail to fill the security gap and reorient our security capabilities away from F-22s and other twentieth-century kinetic weapons, the future could be very grim. Many of our actions designed to *produce* security could, as we've seen, have the opposite effect and *consume* it instead.

In the end, sustainable security in particular areas can only be established by people who live there. The most that outsiders can do is to establish safe spaces, through setting preliminary conditions, in order to lift the pall of fear so that people can freely determine their own futures.

At present, the cost of global peacekeeping is equivalent to 0.55 percent of the U.S. defense budget. This could easily be doubled while still leaving resources available for tackling poverty and climate change. Indeed, the capacities locked up in the defense industry—those thousands of people designing and building F-22s—are uniquely appropriate for the technical challenges of saving energy and developing renewable sources of energy. Far from being an important source of jobs, the production of baroque systems like the F-22 actually diverts skills and know-how and prevents the kinds of investment that could create more jobs in industries that are environmentally and economically sustainable.

So what is the ultimate weapon? It is a mindset that recognizes the essential equality of human lives. This sounds obvious, but in war zones, local civilians are not treated as though they are as important as civilians in the nations whose forces are fighting on their soil or indeed as important as the forces themselves. Force protection comes before civilian protection.

Northern Ireland is instructive in this regard because, in effect, it was involved in a "new war" on British territory. The British government could not bomb Belfast. It could not even have sent drones had the technology been available. When, in 1969, British troops were first sent to Northern Ireland, they did not sufficiently appreciate this. They were experienced in colonial counterinsurgencies and they did not understand the difference between Aden, where they had been deployed most recently, and Belfast. As one soldier put it:

> We weren't governed by the same rules that we were in Ireland. The lads over there [in Aden] could be a lot rougher, a lot harder because we never had the newspapers there and we never had the Press there or anyone else who could see what we were doing. It made a lot of difference because you were given a freer hand right across the board.[7]

During the first few years, the army failed to protect the nationalist community from house burnings and expulsions, which stimulated the militarization of the IRA. The British military used interrogation and intelligence techniques developed in colonial wars that were later ruled illegitimate by the European Court of Human Rights, and it used excessive force, most notoriously in breaking up IRA-established "no-go" areas and on Bloody Sunday, January 30, 1972, when the Parachute Regiment fired on a crowd and killed thirteen people.[8] During the bloodiest period of the conflict, from 1969 to 1974, some 188 people were killed by security forces; 65 percent of those killed were unarmed civilians.[9]

In 1974, a new policy known as normalization, criminalization, or Ulsterization was adopted. Police were to be primarily responsible for dealing with insurgents, and captured terrorists were to be treated as criminals rather than enemies. They were to be tried and given the same status in prison as ordinary criminals. The job of the armed forces was to support the police. Army bases were often co-located with police stations, rather like what Petraeus did in Baghdad. This approach lasted until the Good Friday Agreement of April 1998 largely ended the conflict. But that was after thirty years. The conflict in Northern Ireland lasted as long as it did because the British gov-

ernment and army treated it initially as a traditional war when it was-
n't; it was a question of human security. Conventional military force
made the situation worse. The recovery of trust within the province
and between Britain and Ireland required more than a generation.
In other parts of the world, where the conditions of human insecurity
are much more immediately and generally life-threatening, we cannot tolerate a strategy that requires twenty-five years and several complete changes of course before it becomes effective.

We have to see ourselves as part of the human community—we
cannot be rougher with Afghans and Pakistanis than we would be
with British and Americans. Everything else follows from this understanding, including the ways in which we address what seem to
be more traditional issues like relations with Russia, China, Iran,
and North Korea. It is a profound cognitive shift, no easier for the
Pentagons and ministries of defense of the world than for peace activists, NGOs, and academics. Security in the twenty-first century
is different.

■

When Kaldor called Beebe from her desk at the London School of
Economics to discuss the final draft of this book, he was sitting in
his living room in Luanda, Angola. The generator was grinding outside as it did most days of the week due to lack of power infrastructure in a town where more than 4 million people vie for electricity
from a grid constructed for 400,000. That was not the only noise
Beebe had to get used to living in Luanda. There was also the gas
line that stretched half a mile long. On the day that Kaldor called,
it was, for whatever reason, a light day—there were only some thirty-
five cars waiting to fill up. As they waited, music blared, horns were
honked with impatience, engines without mufflers backfired and
were goosed in frustration, and the stench of exhaust mixed with

the general humidity. The gas line makes for an easy target for local street vendors attempting to sell everything from sunglasses to curtain rods. They range in age from eight or nine to upwards of thirty or forty—old by Angolan standards. The port of Luanda is notorious for corruption and pilferage: the vendors' goods almost certainly came from there.

Sometimes when Beebe was working on the book, he interrupted his writing to stretch his legs. The guard at his house was a courteous older gentlemen who promptly struggled to get up to unlatch the gate. He was wobbly and ill with cholera. Beebe asked him why he didn't stay home and care for himself, but the answer was obvious: "I need the money and have been told if I miss work I'll be fired." Outside the house, a child and an older man often took turns with a dog in sifting through the trash. Down the street, a few kids typically washed cars—on this day, BMW X5s, a Land Rover, and a Mercedes—while other kids played in the muddy, brackish water pool the car washers had created.

Beebe was used to running early in the mornings, before the cars made it unbearable to breathe, along the Rua Houari Boumedienne, a street commonly referred to as "Embassy Row." The street sits upon a bluff overlooking the harbor of Luanda and the "Ilha"— a long finger of land where most of the high end restaurants and night clubs for the nuevo riche are situated. At first glance, it is a beautiful sight. But not always up close: at one end is an area known as the Serpentine. There, as you look down the steep footpaths snaking their way from the bottom to the top of the bluff, you can see garbage littering every step. People sleep in the trash with no cover other than whatever cardboard or plastic or tin they can pull over themselves as protection from the elements. At the other end of Rua Houari Boumedienne is more garbage, but here people pick through the rubbish in search of a meal, never minding that someone might be defecating or urinating immediately nearby. Beebe usually saw a couple of children no more than two years old sitting in the dirt or mud quietly, wide-eyed, watching the street and the many stray dogs.

As a Westerner (and a military officer), Beebe has been taught that exercise is healthy and promotes longevity. Both of Beebe's grandfathers lived to be almost 100; he hopes to do the same. Yet, the people he encountered on his run aspire to live through one more day. Beebe traded an hour of temporary discomfort (he doesn't like running) for the prospect of longevity; meanwhile, the people on the street had mortgaged their entire futures for themselves and their families to survive another day. Luanda is not Africa's poorest city, nor is Angola its most damaged nation. Yet, the daily reality for millions here is an almost unbearable struggle for simple survival. This reality of the voiceless populations of the world was part of the motivation for this book. It is a small scenario played out across many parts of the world that most Westerners have never heard of—if they see them it will likely be from within the comforts of an elite establishment that will shield them from the reality of those struggling for survival in the back alleys and trash dumps just out of view. When people live in desperation, uncertain of life from one day to the next, any offer of a better life for their children becomes desirable. Those digging through the garbage may have nowhere to call home but more often than not do have access to satellite television and can see that others have it far better than they do. They don't know why that should be so, or how it can be justified that one life should be so different from another, valued so differently, just because of where a child was born.

The ambition of a human-security approach is the creation of the conditions for sustainable development benefiting the whole of society—elites and common citizens alike. To believe in the merits of a human-security approach you don't have to believe that everyone is good, simply that in a secure context most people have a vested interest in continued security, and that that makes it easier to marginalize and arrest the bad guys without creating more bad guys in the process. Our world is irrevocably interconnected: if we continue down the current path, discounting the conditions that create instability in faraway places such as Mogadishu and Port Harcourt, we are creating our enemies for the future.

Many will take offense to this book—on both the defense side and the humanitarian side. Some will blame us for wanting to beat swords into plowshares, while others will insist that we've opened the door to a sinister military invasion of humanitarian space. Neither allegation is accurate. We hope what we've introduced is the possibility of a new language to find common ground between both sides, and that the idea of "both sides" might soon be consigned to the lexicon of dated twentieth-century concepts.

The language of human security offers a common security vocabulary for the twenty-first century. With this book, we have attempted to shift focus from how the West defines what is "right" for the developing world and international security to what people in the developing world are saying is "relevant" for their security. The twenty-first century will no more be a replay of the twentieth century than the twentieth century was a replay of the nineteenth. The strategic Cold War algebra of counting planes and tanks and ascertaining military budgets must be swapped for a discrete calculus based on the conditions underlying instability, in which there is no smart bomb or bomber that will offer a solution, and no room to squabble over traditional roles. There is no ultimate weapon of war in twentieth-century terms that will defeat the hybrid threats of the future. The ultimate weapons of the twenty-first century are, in fact, not weapons in the military sense at all.

ACKNOWLEDGMENTS

Many people, too numerous to mention, helped us in writing this book and in influencing our ideas, especially those people that we have met in places such as Africa, the Balkans, the Caucasus, Iraq and Afghanistan who know what it means to experience insecurity.

We would like to thank, first of all, our editor, Clive Priddle and everyone at PublicAffairs who have been so helpful and encouraging in the production of this book.

We also want to thank Mary Kaldor's students who enthusiastically rallied round to provide research assistance. In particular, this book could not have been written without the help of Marika Theros, who arranged interviews, coordinated research assistance and collated research material on Afghanistan, intelligence and communications, training, the US defence industry and budget, Iran, North Korea and Blackwater. Others who helped us greatly included: Stefan Bauchowitz, for research on Chinese security policy, human security indicators in Africa, and piracy; Svenja Petersen for researching the actors in the ICC and Kyoto and the backgrounds to the terrorists involved in the London bombings; Hande Ozhabes for finding quotations about the Cold War and about sovereignty; Janis Dirveiks for research on Russian security thinking; and Madeleine Lyons, for collecting material on private security companies. Domenika Spyratou, Mary Kaldor's personal assistant, also played an invaluable role in helping with appointments, travel arrangements, emails, footnotes, and almost everything else.

We are very grateful to everyone who agreed to be interviewed for this book. They included John Podesta, Laryy Korb and others at the Center for American Progress, Ylber Bajaktari, a friend from Kosovo and also a member of General Petraeus's team in Iraq, Danielle Pletka from the American Enterprise Institute, General Petraeus, General McCaffrey, Jon Cavanagh and John Feffer of the Institute for Policy Studies, Ambassador Pickering, Peter Singer of the Brookings Institution, Andrew Exum and John Nagl at the Centre for New American Security, Sherri Kraham, Thomas Kelly, Alicia Mandaville at the Millennium Challenge Corporation, Ambassador Neumann of the Academy of Diplomacy, Doug Brooks, International Peace Operations, Jef Hofsgard, Vice President for International Operations, Boeing Corporation, General David Barno and faculty at the National Defense University; and Major-General Andrew Salmon.

Our thinking benefited greatly from our colleagues and the environments in which we worked. Although militaries are often times painted as stale and adverse to change, this was not the case during Shannon Beebe's time on US Army general staff. Rather, it was here he received encouragement to explore different ideas and "solutions not yet sought". Special thanks are in order to the Institute for National Security Studies in Colorado Springs, Colorado, and the Army Environmental Policy Institute for sponsoring the lion's share of Shannon's research in the Congo on environmental security which helped shape his thinking on human security. Other members of the US Army staff deserving special recognition are Lieutenant General John F. Kimmons, Mr. Bill Speer, Mr. Eric Kraemer, Mr. Barry Hughes, Lieutenant Colonels, Orlando Pacheco, Will Whatley, John Erwin, and Paul Ross. Numerous officers and civilians at Africa Command (AFRICOM). Staff encouraged discussions on how best to implement a human security approach such as Mr. Paul Saxton, Mr. Terry Ford, Major Generals Richard Sherlock, and Edward Leacock. Others which provided solid critiques and support for this work were Dr. Kent Butts, US Army War College, Dr. Dan Henk, US Air Force War College, Geoff Dabelko Woodrow Wilson Center, and Ambassador Princeton Lyman, Council of Foreign Relations. Thanks are also in order to numerous NGOs and devoted humanitarians within these organizations to extend a hand across traditional boundaries to understand how there is far more to be accomplished working together than working against one another. Special thanks to those at the World Wildlife Fund USA, Wildlife Conservation Society, Greenpeace USA, International Conservation Caucus Foundation, Interaction, Project HOPE, Water Advocates, and Institute for Multi-track Diplomacy. A special thanks to Sherri Goodman and the Center for Naval Analysis Corporation for being included in many of their discussions on climate change and security.

Many of the concepts of human security and, in particular, the principles came out of many exciting discussions with members of the Human Study Group, which reports to Javier Solana, the former EU High Representative for Common and Foreign Security Policy. We are immensely grateful to Dr Solana and also to the distinguished members of the Study Group including Ulrich Albrecht (Free University of Berlin), Christine Chinkin (LSE), Gemma Collantes Celador (City University), Stefanie Flechtner (Freidrich Ebert Stiftung), Marlies Glasius (University of Amsterdam), Kimmo Kiljunen (Finnish Parliament), Jan Klabbers (University of Helsinki), Jenny Kuper (LSE), Sonja Licht (Centre for Political Excellence, Belgrade), Flavio Lotti (Peace Table, Perugia), Klaus Reinhardt (former NATO Commander in Kosovo), Genevieve Schmeder (Conservatoire des Arts et Metiers), Pavel Seifter (former foreign policy advisor to President Vaclav Havel and Czech Ambassador to

London), Narcis Serra (former Spanish Minister of Defence and Vice Prime Minister) and Gert Weisskirchen (German Bundestag), as well as advisors to the Study Group including Ana Gomez (European parliament) Robert Cooper (Chief of Staff to Dr Solana) Alex Rondos (foreign policy advisor to George Papandreou) and Major-General Andrew Salmon. The human security team at LSE helped coordinate the work of the study group and provide crucial background research; they include, as well as the students mentioned above, Mary Martin, Yahia Said, Vesna Bojicic-Dzelilovic, Denisa Kostovicova, Iavor Rangelov as well as others. Finally, the seeds for human security were planted during Mary Kaldor's time in the Helsinki Citizens Assembly (HCA) and through continuing discussions with others active in the HCA particularly Mient Jan Faber. We would also like to thank Robin Luckham, who read and commented on parts of the manuscript.

A special thanks goes to Peter Pringle for much needed advice and support and for introducing us to Clive. And, of course, our families especially Julian Perry Robinson who picked up mistaken metaphors and misplaced commas, as well as Josh Kaldor-Robinson and Oliver Robinson who discussed the title and the contents.

The book, of course, is entirely our responsibility writing in a personal capacity. None of the views in this book can be attributed to anyone other than Mary Kaldor and Shannon Beebe. In particular, they cannot be attributed to the US Army or the Department of Defense.

NOTES

Chapter 1: Introduction

1. United Nations Development Programme (UNDP) *Human Development Report 1994* (New York: Oxford University Press, 1994).

2. UN (2005). The High Level Panel on Threats, Challenges and Change *In Larger Freedom: Towards Development, Security and Human Rights for All*. Report to the Secretary-General, http://www.un.org/largerfreedom/contents.htm.

3. *Human Security Report: War and Peace in the 21st Century*. Human Security Centre, University of British Columbia, Canada, Oxford: Oxford University Press, 2005; *The Responsibility to Protect. Report of the International Commission on Intervention and State Sovereignty*, 2001.

4. Sen, Amartya, (2003) "Development, rights and human security" in Sen and Ogata, *Human Security Now*, Commission on Human Security Report (New York), 2003: 8-9.

5. http://www.whitehouse.gov/the-press-office/remarks-president-address-nation-way-forward-afghanistan-and-pakistan.

6. http://www.cfr.org/publication/21000/us_policy_in_afghanistan.html?breadcrumb=%2Fpublication%2Fby_type%2Ftranscript.

7. Quoted in Andrew Exum "The conflict in Central Asia will likely mark the end of the current era of counterinsurgency," *Boston Review*, January/February 2010.

Chapter 2

1. These numbers are based on the figures collected by the Research and Documentation Center in Sarajevo. http://www.idc.org.ba/.

(At the time of the war, estimates provided by international agencies were much higher.)

2. Susan Woodward, Balkan *Tragedy: Chaos and Dissolution after the Cold War* (Washington DC: Brookings Institution, 1995).

3. IMF, *Democratic Republic of Congo Selected Issues and Statistical Appendix*. July, 3 2001.

4. Amnesty International, *Democratic Republic of Congo: "Our brothers who help kill us": Economic Exploitation and Human Rights Abuse in the East*. AFR 62/010/2003, March 31, 2003.

5. http://hdrstats.undp.org/countries/country_fact_sheets/cty_fs_COD.html

6. David Rieff, *Slaughterhouse: Bosnia and the failure of the West* (London: Vintage Books, 1996).

7. Hugh/Grundig, Frank/Zorick, Ethan R., "Marching At the Pace of the Slowest." *Political Studies* 49 (2004): 438–461; Oberthuer, Sebastian: *The Kyoto Protocol*. (Germany: Springer-Verlag, 1999); Andresen, Steinar/Gulbrandsen, Lars H., "NGO Influence in the Implementation of the Kyoto Protocol: Compliance, Flexibility Mechanisms, and Sinks," *Global Environmental Politics* 4, No. 4 (2004): 54-75.

8. Glasius, Marlies: *The International Criminal Court: A Global Civil Society Achievement* (London: Routledge, 2005).

Chapter 3

1. 1965 is the year that ground troops were officially sent to Vietnam, although many would argue that the war began much earlier and that the U.S. presence in the form of so-called military advisers was already very significant.

2. John A. Nagl, *Learning to eat soup with a knife: Counterinsurgency lessons from Malaya and Vietnam* (Chicago: University of Chicago Press, 2005) p.49.

3. Richard Gabriel and Paul Savage, *Crisis in Command* (New York: Hill and Wang, 1978).

4. Quoted in Nagl, op.cit. p.172.

5. Harry Summers, *On Strategy: A Critical Analysis of the Vietnam War* (Novato, California: Presidio Press, 1982).

6. *Wall Street Journal* February 23 1990.

7. Zbigniew Brzezinski "Cold War and Its Aftermath," *Foreign Affairs*, Vol. 71, No. 4 (Fall, 1992), pp. 31-49.

8. Project for a New American Century, *Rebuilding America's Defenses: Strategy, Forces and Resources for a New Century*, Washington DC, September, 2000.

9. Quoted in Nagl, op.it.

10. November 27, 1995. http://www.cnn.com/US/9511/bosnia_speech/speech.html.

11. "Bosnia: So far, So Good," *Defence Issues* 11, 5 (1996).

12. Richard Caplan, "International Diplomacy and the Crisis in Kosovo," *International Affairs*, 74, 4 (October 1998), p. 752.

13. Some Western leaders claim that they were taken by surprise by the accelerated ethnic cleansing. But it was quite clear that this was likely to happen. It was reported by *The Times* of London that Western intelligence knew about a plan called Operation Horseshoe as early as September, although this has never been substantiated. Reportedly, the Yugoslav General, Sreten Lukic, told members of the Kosovo verification mission: "Give us a week and we will clean the terrorists out of Kosovo." Likewise, Seselj, the leader of the Serbian Radical Party and deputy prime minister of Serbia, warned on television, one week before the bombing began, that "not a single Albanian would remain if NATO bombed." Whether Operation Horseshoe existed or not, it is evident from the pattern of logistical arrangements made for the deportation of Albanians and from the coordination of actions by the Yugoslav army, the police, and paramilitary groups that this huge expulsion of people was systematic and deliberately planned. See the International Independent Commission on Kosovo: The Kosovo Report Oxford University Press, 2000.

14. *NATO Military Briefing*, April 1, 1999. http://www.pbs.org/newshour/bb/europe/jan-june99/nato_4-1.html.

15. *Doctrine of the International Community* at the Economic Club, Chicago. http://www.number-10.gov.uk/output/Page1297.asp.

16. *New York Review of Books*, June 10, 1999.

17. "Notes for a speech to the Empire Club," Toronto, Department of Foreign Affairs, *Statement* 99/43, June 28, 1999.

Chapter 4

1. *President George W. Bush Addresses the Council on Foreign Relations*, December 7, 2005. http://www.cfr.org/publication/9355/.

2. President George W. Bush, *President Bush Announces Major Combat Operations in Iraq Have Ended: Remarks by President Bush from the USS Abraham Lincoln.* May 1, 2003.

3. Max Boot, "The New American Way of War," *Foreign Affairs* July/August 2003.

4. Donald H. Rumsfeld, Testimony to the Senate Armed Services Committee, July 9, 2003.

5. Ahmed S. Hashim, *The Sunni Insurgency in Iraq* (Newport, Rhode Island: Center for Naval War Studies, August 15, 2003).

6. Yahia Said, "Civil Society in Iraq," in Helmut Anheier, Marlies Glasius and Mary Kaldor. *Global Civil Society 2004/5* (London: Sage, 2004) p.6.

7. Ashraf Ghani and Clare Lockhart, *Fixing failed states: a framework for rebuilding a fractured world* (Oxford: Oxford University Press, 2008).

8. Quoted in Lawrence Freedman, "The Transformation of Strategic Affairs," *Adelphi Papers* 379, 2006.

9. Condoleeza Rice "In the National Interest" *Foreign Affairs* 79, No.1 (2000): 53.

10. United States Institute for Peace, *Securing Afghanistan: Challenges for the Next Administration*. Washington DC, November 2008.

11. Abu Musab al-Zarqawi, a Jordanian militant who had fought with the mujahideen in Afghanistan, had established in 2001 a small group, Ansar Al-Islam, that had a camp in the autonomous northern part of Iraq. Zarqawi joined with the more extremist Islamist groups in Iraq after the invasion; in 2004, he pledged allegiance to Osama bin Laden and renamed his organization Al-Qaeda in Mesopotamia or Al-Qaeda in the Land of Two Rivers.

12. Austin Long, "The Anbar Awakening" *Survival*. Vol 50, No2 (2008): 67–94.

13. Prof Gilbert Burnham MD, Prof Riyadh Lafta MD, Shannon Doocy PhD, Les Roberts PhD, "Mortality after the 2003 invasion of Iraq: a cross-sectional cluster sample survey." *The Lancet,* Volume 368, Issue 9545 (2006): 1421–1428

14. UNAMA, *Afghanistan: Annual Report on Protection of Civilians in Armed Conflict,* 2008.

15. CRS, Report for Congress, Order Code RL33851, January 26, 2007, Rhoda Margesson, *Afghan Refugees: Current Status and Future Prospects.*

16. Mundt, Alex and Schmeidl, Susanne, "The Failure to Protect: Battle-Affected IDPs in Southern Afghanistan." The Brookings Institution, June 22, 2009

17. Ricks, *op.cit.* p.34.

18. *Ibid.* p.7.

19. Department of the Army and United States Marine, Corps "Counterinsurgency. Field Manual No 3-24," *Marine Corps Warfighting Publications* No 3-33.5, Washington DC, December 2006.

20. *Ibid.* p. 1-27.

21. Kilcullen, *op.cit.* p.182.

22. Commander, NATO International Security Assistance Forces, Afghanistan, US Forces, Afghanistan, *Commander's Initial Assessment* 30 August 2009.

23. Peter Singer, *Wired for War: The Robotics Revolution and Conflict in the 21st Century* (Washington DC: Brookings Institution, 2009).

24. *Ibid.* p. 223.

25. *Ibid.* p. 34.

26. Interview with Kaldor.

Chapter 5

1. Quoted in Richard Norton Taylor, "Iraq:the Legacy – Ill equipped, poorly trained, and mired in a bloody mess," *The Guardian*, April 17 2009.

2. Reidar Vissar, "Historical Myths of a Divided Iraq," *Survival*, Vol 50, Issue 2 (2008): 95–106.

3. Quoted on Jonathan Steele. *Defeat: Why they lost Iraq* (London: I.B.Tauris, 2008): 182.

4. Interview, March 2009.

5. Michel Wievorka, *La Violence* (Paris: Balland, 2004).

6. Quoted in Victoria K.Holt and Tobias C.Berkman, *The Impossible Mandate? Military Preparedness, the Responsibility to Protect and Modern Peace Operations.* The Henry L. Stimson Center, 2006, p.147.

7. *Ibid.* p.174.

8. http://www.sl.undp.org/2_focus/afd_end_yr_rpt07.pdf.

9. http://www.globalhumanitarianassistance.org/.

10. David Keen *Complex Emergencies*, (Cambridge: Polity Press, 2008) :154.

11. *Human Security Now: Final Report of the Commission on Human Security.* Co-Chairs Sadako Ogata and Amertya Sen, United Nations, May 1 2003, http://humansecurity-chs.org/finalreport/index.html.

Chapter 6

1. Rebecca Grant, *Global Deterrence.* Lexington Institute, February 6, 2009. http://www.lexingtoninstitute.org/global-deterrence-the-role-of-the-f-22.

2. http://www.humansecuritygateway.com/.

3. http://www.arab-hdr.org/.

4. http://www.unodc.org/unodc/crime_cicp_survey_countries.html.

5. http://www.internal-displacement.org.

6. http://www.unhcr.org/4a375c426.html.

7. Guha-Sapir, D. and D. Hargitt and Phoyois. *Thirty Years of Natural Disasters 1974-2005: The Numbers* (Louvain: Presses Univesitaires de Louvain, 2004). The database distinguishes between two categories of disasters: natural disasters and technological disasters. Natural disasters are classified into twelve predefined types: drought, earthquake, epidemic, extreme temperature, famine, flood, insect infestation, slides, volcano, wave/surge, wildfire, and windstorm. Technological disasters are classified into three predefined types: industrial accident, miscellaneous accident, and transport accident.

8. Owen, Taylor (2004), "Challenges and opportunities for defining and measuring human security," *Disarmament Forum* [Human Rights, Human Security and Disarmament] 3: 15–24.

9. Documented by Shaun McCarthy, *The Function of Intelligence in Crisis Management* (Farnham: Ashgate Publishing, 1998).

10. Martin, David and Walcott, John, *Best Laid Plans: The Inside Story of America's War Against Terrorism* (New York: Harper and Row, 1988).

11. Gates, Robert, Speech delivered to the Association of American Universities (Washington DC), April 14, 2008. Available at: http://www.defenselink.mil/speeches/speech.aspx?speechid=1228.

12. http://concerned.anthropologists.googlepages.com/.

13. http://www.ushmm.org/maps/projects/darfur/.

14. Zaccaro, Sabina, "Rights: Satellite Data Aid Human Rights Campaigns." *Inter-Press Service*, September 3, 2007.

15. http://www.eyesondarfur.org/about.html.

16. http://shr.aaas.org/geotech/.

17. http://www.fews.net/Pages/default.aspx.

18. A report for the European Space Agency found that the biggest gap in human security operation was in telecommunications. See European Space Agency *European Space and Human Security Working Group, Paris, 2006.*

19. The story is told in Genevieve Schmeder "Equipment and Resources," in Marlies Glasius and Mary Kaldor, *A Human Security Doctrine for Europe* (London: Routledge, 2005).

20. http://www.ushahidi.com/.

21. Albon, Christopher, "Ushahidi deploys in the DRC." *War and Health*, November 7, 2008. available at: http://warandhealth.com/ushahidi-deploys-in-the-drc/.

22. Dickinson, Elizabeth, "Net Effect: Neighborhood Watch." *Foreign Policy*, January/February 2009. Available at: http://www.foreignpolicy.com/story/cms .php?story_id=4601.

23. http://labs.aljazeera.net/warongaza.

24. Stockholm International Peace Research Institute, *SIPRI Yearbook 2009: Armament, Disarmament and Security* (Oxford: Oxford University Press, 2009).

25. Robert Gates, "A Balanced Strategy," *Foreign Affairs*, Vol 88, No 1 (2009).

26. Major General Robert H. Scales, "The Second Learning Revolution," *Military Review*, January – February 2006, p40.

27. According to Max Boot, the *New York Times* report left out the phrase 'a bit' thereby exaggerating American difficulties. See Max Boot, *op.cit.*

28. Anheier, Helmut, Glasius, Marlies, and Kaldor, Mary, *Global Civil Society 2001* (Oxford: Oxford University Press, 2001).

29. Peter Singer, *Corporate warriors :the rise of the privatized military industry* (Ithaca: Cornell University Press, 2001).

30. Economist.com, "Blackwater's Dark Heart," August 21, 2009.

31. Jeremy Scahill, *Blackwater: the Rise of the World's Most Powerful Mercenary Army* (New York: Nation Books, 2007) :24.

32. Colonel Mark Cancian, "In Defense of Security Contractors." http://experts.foreignpolicy.com/node/15019.

33. http://www.globalsecurity.org/military/library/policy/dod/qdr-2006-report .htm.

34. Jermy Scahill, *op.cit.*

35. Jeremy Scahill, *Blackwater: the Rise of the World's Most Powerful Mercenary Army*. Nation Books: New York, 2007, pp 57.

36. Associated Press, "House Passes Bill That Would Hike Penalties for U.S. Security Contractors in Iraq," October 4, 2007.

37. http://www.gibsondunn.com/publications/pages/NewStatusofForces AgreementSubjectsGovernmentContractorstoIraqiLaw.aspx.

38. James Risen and Mark Mazzetti, "C.I.A. Said to Use Outsiders to Put Bombs on Drones." August 20, 2009. Accessible at: http://www.nytimes.com/2009/08/21/us/21intel.html.

39. Patrap Chatterjee and A.C. Thompson, "Private Contractors and Torture at Abu Ghraib." *Corpwatch*, May 7, 2004. http://www.corpwatch.org/.

40. Thomas A. Schweich, "The Pentagon is muscling in everywhere. Its time to stop mission creep." *Washington Post* December 21, 2008 (Schweich was Ambassador for anti-drug policy in Afghanistan under the Bush Administration).

41. *The Baroque Arsenal* (New York: Hill and Wang, 1982).

42. Statement of Michael Sullivan, Director of Defense Acquisition and Sourcing Management "Defense Acquisitions: DOD Must prioritize Its Weapons Systems Acquisitions and Balane them with Availble Resources," GAO 2008.

43. Frida Berrigan, *Entrenched, Embedded and Here to Stay: The Pentagon's Expansion will be Bush's Lasting Legacy,* New America Foundation, May 27, 2008. http://www.newamerica.net/publications/articles/2008/entrenched_embedded_ and_here_stay_7228.

44. The American Academy of Diplomacy, "A Foreign Affairs Budget for the Future: Fixing the Crisis in Diplomatic Readiness," October 2008, p4, available at: http://www.academyofdiplomacy.org/publications/FAB_report _2008.pdf.

45. Hillary Clinton's Confirmation Hearing Transcript for Secretary of State, January 13, 2009, available at: http://www.scribd.com/doc/10323001/Hillary -Clinton-Confirmation-Transcript-for-Secretary-of-State-January-13-2009.

46. J. Anthony Holmes, "Where are the Civilians: How to Rebuild the U.S. Foreign Service," *Foreign Affairs*, Vol 88, No 1, (2009).

47. *A Unified Security Budget for the United States FY 2009*, Institute for Policy Studies, September 2008.

48. *A Human Security Doctrine for Europe*: *The Barcelona Report of the Study Group on Europe's Security Capabilities*, Barcelona, 2004, https://www.lse.ac.uk/ Depts/global/Publications/HumanSecurityDoctrine.pdf.

Chapter 7

1. *Budget Press Briefing* (Arlington, VA), as prepared for delivery by Secretary of Defense Robert Gates, 6 April 2009; access: http://www.defenselink.mil/ speeches/speech.aspx?speechid=1341.

2. Robert Gates, *Foreign Affairs* (2009), *op.cit.*

3. Robert Kagan, *The Return of History and the End of Dreams* (London: Atlantic, 2008): 1.

4. Ivan Krastev "Sovereign democracy, Russian-style," *Open Democracy* 16 November 2006. http://www.opendemocracy.net/globalization-institutions_ government/sovereign_democracy_4104.jsp

5. Quoted in *Ibid*.

6. Bates Gill, *Rising Star: China's New Security Diplomacy* (Washington DC: Brookings Institution, 2007), p.107.

7. *Kommersant,* December 25, 2008. http://www.kommersant.ru/doc-y.aspx?
DocsID=1099153 [Newspaper claimed to have acquired a copy of the draft
strategy].

8. *Kommersant,* December 25, 2008 (http://www.kommersant.ru/doc-y.aspx?
DocsID=1099153)

9. *Ibid.*

10. Rus: http://www.scrf.gov.ru/documents/1.html. The newest edition ap-
proved by the Presidential Decree No.24, 10 January 2000.

11. http://eurasianhome.org/doc/declaration_on_fifth_anniversary_of_shang-
hai_cooperation_organization.doc.

12. Li, Nan, "PLA Conservative Nationalism." in: Finkelstein, D. Flanagan,
S. & Marti, M. *(ed) The People's Liberation Army and China in Transition*
(Washington DC: National Defense University, 2003): 69-89.

13. SIPRI database http://www.sipri.org/databases/milex.

14. "China's Foreign and Security Policy: Partner or Rival?" in Bergsten, C.
F, Bates Gill, Nicholas Lardy and Derek Mitchell: *China: the Balance Sheet,
What the world needs to know now about the Emerging Superpower* (New York:
PublicAffairs, 2006): 136

15. Babak Rahimi, "Cyberdissent: The Internet in Revolutionary Iran," *Middle East Review of International Affairs,* Vol.7, No3, September 2003, http://
meria.idc.ac.il/journal/2003/issue3/jv7n3a7.html.

16. http://www.allacademic.com/meta/p212142_index.html.

17. http://www.hrw.org/en/news/2008/04/14/north-korea-s-transformation-
famine-aid-and-markets.

18. BBC, April 25, 2006.

19. Hillary Mann, "US Diplomacy with Iran: The Limits of Tactical Engagement," Statement to the Subcommittee on National Security and Foreign Affairs,
Committee on Government Oversight and Reform, US House of Representatives, November 7, 2007

20. Zakaria, Fareed, "Tag-Teaming the Mullahs," *Newsweek,* 6 December
2004, p37.

21. The Iran Nuclear Policy Group, *How to Approach the Iran Nuclear
Dilemma: White Paper by the Iran Nuclear Policy Group of the American Foreign Policy Project,* the American Foreign Policy Project, 9 April 2009, accessible at: http://americanforeignpolicy.org/.

22. Salehi-Isfahani, Djavad , "Iran Sanctions: Who Really Wins?" Brookings
Institution, October 12, 2009, accessed at: http://www.brookings.edu/opinions/
2009/0930_iran_sanctions_salehi_isfahani.aspx?p=1.

23. Abbas Milani, "U.S. Foreign Policy and the Future of Democracy in Iran," *The Washington Quarterly* 28(3): 2005 pp.41–56.

24. The Iran Nuclear Policy Group, *How to Approach the Iran Nuclear Dilemma: White Paper by the Iran Nuclear Policy Group of the American Foreign Policy Project*, the American Foreign Policy Project, April 9, 2009, accessible at: http://americanforeignpolicy.org/.

25. http://www.cdi.org/north-korea/north-korea-crisis.pdf.

26. http://www.nytimes.com/2009/05/28/world/asia/28korea.html.

27. Council on Foreign Relations, "After Latest Brinksmanship, Engaging North Korea," Interview with Sheila A. Smith, April 6, 2009, accessible at: http://www.cfr.org/publication/19044/after_latest_brinksmanship_engaging_north_korea.html.

28. http://news.bbc.co.uk/1/shared/bsp/hi/pdfs/30_09_09_iiffmgc_report.pdf.

29. Barry Posen, "Command of the Commons: The Military Foundations of US hegemony," *International Security*, Vol 38, No. 1 (2003): 5–46.

Chapter 8

1. "The 13 parasitic and bacterial infections known as the neglected tropical diseases include three soil-transmitted helminth infections (ascariasis, hookworm infection, and trichuriasis), lymphatic filariasis, onchocerciasis, dracunculiasis, schistosomiasis, Chagas' disease, human African trypanosomiasis, leishmaniasis, Buruli ulcer, leprosy, and trachoma. An expanded list could include dengue fever, the treponematoses, leptospirosis, strongyloidiasis, foodborne trematodiases, neurocysticercosis, and scabies, as well as other tropical infections." Peter J. Hotez, David H. Molyneux, Alan Fenwick, Jacob Kumaresan, Sonia Ehrlich Sachs, Jeffrey D. Sachs, and Lorenzo Savioli, The Control of Neglected Tropical Diseases, *New England Journal of Medicine*, 375(10):1018-1027, September 2007.

2. www.activeworlds.com.

Chapter 9

1. Tom Donelly and Gary Schmitt, "How to make a Real Stimulus Take," *Washington Post*, Feb 8, 2009.

2. "Lockheed F-22 Fighter poses Early Test of Obama's Goals," Bloomberg .com March 23, 2009.

3. Mark Bowden, "The Last Ace," *Atlantic Online*, March 2009.

4. *Boston Globe*, March 22 2009.

5. *SIPRI Yearbook 2009: Armaments, Disarmament, and Security* (Oxford: Oxford University Press, 2009).

6. Stathis N. Kalyvas and Laia Balcells, *International System and Technologies of Rebellion: How the Cold War Shaped Internal Conflict*, Unpublished paper, 2008.

7. Quoted in Peter Taylor, *The Brits: The War against the IRA* Bloomsbury, London, 2001.

8. Peter Pringle and Philip Jacobson, *Those are Real bullets, Aren't they?* Fourth Estate, London, 2000.

9. Fionnuala Ní Aoláin, *The Politics of Force: Conflict Management ad State Violence in Northern Ireland*, Blackstaff press, Belfast, 2000.

INDEX

ABOUT THE AUTHORS

Lieutenant Colonel **Shannon D. Beebe** served as the senior Africa analyst at the Pentagon and in Luanda, Angola, where he worked for the United States Embassy.

Mary Kaldor is professor and director of the Centre for the Study of Global Governance, London School of Economics and Political Science. Her books include *The Baroque Arsenal*, *The Imaginary War*, *New and Old Wars*, and *Global Civil Society*. She lives in London, England.

PUBLICAFFAIRS is a publishing house founded in 1997. It is a tribute to the standards, values, and flair of three persons who have served as mentors to countless reporters, writers, editors, and book people of all kinds, including me.

I. F. STONE, proprietor of *I. F. Stone's Weekly,* combined a commitment to the First Amendment with entrepreneurial zeal and reporting skill and became one of the great independent journalists in American history. At the age of eighty, Izzy published *The Trial of Socrates,* which was a national bestseller. He wrote the book after he taught himself ancient Greek.

BENJAMIN C. BRADLEE was for nearly thirty years the charismatic editorial leader of *The Washington Post.* It was Ben who gave the *Post* the range and courage to pursue such historic issues as Watergate. He supported his reporters with a tenacity that made them fearless, and it is no accident that so many became authors of influential, best-selling books.

ROBERT L. BERNSTEIN, the chief executive of Random House for more than a quarter century, guided one of the nation's premier publishing houses. Bob was personally responsible for many books of political dissent and argument that challenged tyranny around the globe. He is also the founder and was the longtime chair of Human Rights Watch, one of the most respected human rights organizations in the world.

·   ·   ·

For fifty years, the banner of Public Affairs Press was carried by its owner Morris B. Schnapper, who published Gandhi, Nasser, Toynbee, Truman, and about 1,500 other authors. In 1983 Schnapper was described by *The Washington Post* as "a redoubtable gadfly." His legacy will endure in the books to come.

Peter Osnos, *Founder and Editor-at-Large*